LEA
MOTIVATION

LEADERSHIP &

MOTIVATION

THE KEY TO ACHIEVING
WHAT YOU WANT IN LIFE

ELVIN VONG

Pelanduk
Publications

Published by
Pelanduk Publications (M) Sdn. Bhd.
(Co. No: 113307-W)
12 Jalan SS13/3E, Subang Jaya Industrial Estate,
47500 Subang Jaya, Selangor, Malaysia.
e-mail: *rusaone@tm.net.my*
website: *www.pelanduk.com*

Perpustakaan Negara Malaysia   Cataloguing-in-Publication Data

Vong, Elvin
    Leadership & motivation : the key to achieving what you
    want in life / Elvin Vong.
    ISBN 978-967-978-960-7
    1. Achievement motivation. 2. Motivation (Psychology)
    3. Leadership – Psychological aspects. I. Title.
    158.1

Printed and bound in Malaysia.

Printed by:UG Press Sdn Bhd

CONTENTS

Foreword I

Foreword II

Acknowledgements

Introduction

I   BELIEF SYSTEMS   *1*
- How to Tap into your Potential
- Visualization
- Negative Belief Systems
- Empowering and Creating Positive
  Belief Systems

II   BE MOTIVATED! FEEL INSPIRED!   *27*
- Is Motivation Permanent?
- What is Motivation?
- What is Inspiration?
- Journey to the Destination

- Hope and Expectations
- Failure as a Motivator? Why Not?
- Motivation for Continuous Personal Growth

III   GOALS: YOUR DRIVING FORCE   *51*
- Raise your Acceptance Level
- Four Steps to Achieving your Goals
- Come Up with a Blueprint Plan of What You Want to Achieve
- Take Action on the Plan that You have Set your Mind Upon
- Review Your Plans Periodically and Receive Feedback
- Take Action and Keep Evaluating Your Plan until You Achieve the Desired Results
- SMART Goals
- Stretch Goals to Stretch Your Imagination

IV   DESIRE: FUEL FOR YOUR SUCCESS   *79*
- Letting Go of the Past is Only Possible With Great Desires
- Identifying your Desires
- Pay Attention to your Desires
- How to Make Positive Affirmations
- Allowing your Desires to Take Shape

V   EFFECTIVE LEADERSHIP: THE KEY TO
    GROWTH AND SUSTAINABILITY   105
    • The Vision of the Leader
    • The Art of Persuasion
    • Values

VI   RELATIONSHIPS, TEAMWORK
     AND YOU   129
     • The Role of the Team Leader
     • Reasons Why People Refuse to Work
       in a Team
     • Characteristics of Effective Teams
     • Identity Identifies your Team
     • Four Simple Ways to Achieve
       Effective Teamwork
     • Effective Communication Is Key
     • Call Centre Experience

VII   ACCOUNTABILITY, INTEGRITY AND
      RESPONSIBILITY   153
      • Integrity
      • Why is it Important to have Integrity?
      • Integrity Builds Confidence in People
      • Integrity Influences and Inspires
      • Integrity Creates Solid Reputation and
        Lasting Image
      • Integrity Means Living it in Your Heart
        Before Inspiring Others

- Accountability
- Accountability for the Future
- Responsibility

POSTWORD   175
REFERENCES AND SUGGESTED READING   177
THE AUTHOR   179

FOREWORD I

You are going to enjoy this book! Hardly has any first time author managed to capture the essence of management and leadership so clearly. You can apply the life-changing principles and procedures in your personal, family and business life.

Elvin brings along good leadership, communication, people skill, highly motivated, a self-starter and results driven. He's full of vision and ideas for the continuous growth of people around him.

Additionally, the many examples that were given motivates people to think what is actually possible is not so far fetched as one may think.

In each chapter, Elvin goes straight to the heart of a leadership trait, showing you, through real life examples, the successes and failures of others and how you can apply it in your everyday life.

I heartily recommend this book. It is helpful and easy to read, yet profound in its depth and clarity. Suitable for those who are finding their path, values in life.

SudharSanan Palandy Samy
Senior Manager,
Scicom MSc, Bhd

FOREWORD II

Nothing in this book is complex, unexplained or difficult. Elvin Vong has penned it to help you start off the process to maximize your potential.

I enjoyed reading Chapter Two, where Elvin has given straightforward and adequate examples of "DESIRE". The concept serves as crucial foundation to anyone who wants to be successful.

If you want to be successful in areas of life you desire, read this BOOK!!

Asian bestseller in the making, read it, apply it and enjoy it!! Elvin has penned down his experience and thoughts to help you.

Read this book!! You can count on the tools presented to achieve your GOAL.

Wish I could have read and applied the formula when I was in primary school. It took me many years of reading to learn the same tools packaged in this book.

Don't waste time wondering, apply the tools given by Elvin and share your success with others.

I wish I could have read this book earlier in my career to accelerate my true potential.

Ganesh Muthiah
Manager, Performance Improvement,
NCSI (Malaysia)

ACKNOWLEDGEMENTS

I would like to thank my many colleagues who has helped me while I was working on this book; most notably my mentor Ganesh Muthiah who helped shape me to who I am today. He showed me what was possible and how to strive for more in the correct way. He is always the one to look for advice and motivation.

To Sudharsanan Palandy Samy, who has motivated me all the way throughout my fledgling career, and never allowing me to give up and insisting "THERE IS ALWAYS SOMETHING WE CAN DO".

I would also like to thank Jacinta Lim You Peng for providing me with the support and never ending encouragement during the time that I was working on this book. Without it, this book would have not been possible. You have also helped change the way I look at this world, and more importantly, you changed my world. I hope that with the publication of this book, I too can help change the way others look at things in a more positive mind frame.

To Wilson Law, who has selflessly assisted me countless times, in meeting crucial time lines with regard to the text of this book. I would also like to thank him for providing useful insights and ideas to make this book a reality.

Finally, I would also like to thank my parents for their unwavering support, their encouragement notwithstanding their presence. This book would not have been written without their help.

To the rest of the people whom I fail to mention, allow me to apologize as there are simply too many to mention. You know who you are and I would like to take this opportunity to sincerely thank you for all the support and encouragement that you have given to make this book possible.

INTRODUCTION

Over the last three years, I am fortunate to be working under the tutelage of several very effective leaders who no doubt have left a lasting impression on me. These people are visionaries, selfless and never cease to share the information they have, wanting their fellow beings to learn and know more.

In return, I wish to share what these people have imparted to me and focus my time and energy on doing what makes a positive impact in the lives of people. But along the way, I have also made many mistakes. More than most people I know.

Every success and failure has been an invaluable lesson. I hope to help others not to make the same mistakes. In this book, there are many examples of how renowned leaders struggled in their early years, but only to bounce back, because of their persistence, their determination never to let one failure, ten failures or even a hundred failures dampen their spirit. With this I can say with confidence that you too can succeed.

Here, I want to encourage you to continuously strive to learn to be a better parent, a better sibling, a better husband and of course a better individual. Enjoy the process of learning, give it your best shot, and never forget that no matter what you want to do in life, only you can decide where you want to go.

I
BELIEF SYSTEMS

> *"Our belief has the power to create and the power to destroy"*
> *– Anthony Robbins –*

There is nothing as powerful as the power of commitment, the power of persistence and the power of great desire to get what you want. Have you heard of a person called Roger Bannister? Well, he sure had all these attributes.

Before 1954, nobody had ever run a mile in under four minutes. Nobody believed it could be done as they believed that it was beyond human potential.

Roger Bannister, a 25-year-old medical student from Britain, became the first person who ran the mile in less than four minutes. His remarkable official time was 3 minutes 59 seconds. Before that race, he had been training consistently and had planned to run the mile in less than four minutes. The journey and race was carefully planned and practiced, with the aid of two pacemakers, Chris Brasher and Chris Chataway.

Weeks before the race, Bannister had been training diligently in high winds and cold temperatures. The weather at the track and field was by no means ideal, let alone conducive for breaking records. There were often 15 mph crosswinds with short gusts of up to 25 mph. Initially, Bannister had wanted to give up and call off the race. But there were about 3,000 spectators whom he did not have the heart to disappoint.

During the race, Brasher was his first pacemaker and about 200 yards from the finishing line, Bannister took the lead with a final burst of energy. After he completed the race, he not only dispelled the notion that the four minute mile would never be broken, but also beat his closest rival, Australian athlete John Landy, to the record. In his heart, he had never doubted himself and his abilities.

The best thing is, the year after his achievement, more than 100 people also achieved the same milestone. Why was that so? It was simply because they had a reference they could benchmark themselves against. The Four-Minute Record was no longer a limiting standard for people. People started to believe that they too could run that distance under four minutes.

It is important that when you set your mind to do something, do not let others' negative comments limit your own beliefs. When you think it is possible, you can be sure you will be able to overcome whatever obstacles that stand in your way.

A belief system is a set of core values and firm beliefs that affect our every day decision-making. These values can be classified as a "set of rules" which you live by every single day. If someone told you that he saw a purple elephant that had eight legs in the zoo that day, would you just take his word for it? You would probably question his sanity. This is because your belief system, coupled the references that you have accumulated since young, tell you that elephants are grey and four-legged.

Everybody subscribes to a belief system, regardless whether it helps us to better manage our lives. However, sometimes, one's belief system may have negative impact on one's life. Most people subconsciously take their beliefs for granted and cruise through life unaware that every decision they make will affect them, their closest friends, or even strangers either directly or indirectly.

Fortunately, there is a way in which we can redefine these belief systems into core values that we would like to acquire. As a result, we would be able to see a clearer picture that would help us achieve the fulfilling life that we desire.

When we were born, we knew not what is hot, cold, soft, bright or dark. Through sheer experimentation and, trial and error, we evolve into beings learning to absorb pieces of information, to work with others, move about in the world. As a result, our consciousness is expanded, and we attempt to become what we desire. Note that we must first know what we want before we can determine what we want to become and where we want to go.

To identify your belief system, ask yourself what are the things or values that you hold dear in life. Is it having more money? Being happy? Or having tonnes of friends? Would it be the food we enjoy eating? Creating a warm and loving family? Carving a successful career? All the above are example which you might base your decision-making process on. They provide a foundation for analyzing and classifying your life experiences.

Belief systems vary with age and become more mature in different environment. In our childhood years, we probably believed that Superman existed or that the Tooth Fairy would visit during the night and replace your fallen baby tooth with some money underneath your pillow.

However, as you grow older and become more mature, you would come to realize that these belief systems are not backed by valid references or experiences. You adapt to the new belief systems according to your previous experience. When a particular experience is repeated, it is further reinforced in your belief system. In Thailand, fried grasshoppers and scorpions are considered as one of their finest delicacies and savouring them is very much part of the Thai culture. However, in more developed countries like the United States of America or Australia, this culture is unheard of and diners will lose their appetite if they find out that fried grasshoppers are on the menu!

With the right belief system, an ordinary person can accomplish the most extraordinary things unheard of to many. However, we must be cautioned that holding on to a limited belief system may cripple even the most intelligent.

Have you ever wondered why some people are able to achieve so much in such a short time while others spend their entire lifetime void of any success? Is it because the former were "destined" for stardom? Or was it that they were lucky and befriended the "right" people in their lives?

Why is it that Roger Federer can consistently deliver championship-winning-shots while others simply get knocked out in the first round? What do you think is the reason for Tiger Woods winning Major after Major? Or why do some people resort to violence to solve their problems?

The answer is that these people have incredible sets of belief systems that they follow religiously. These people breathe the same air you and I breathe. What therefore sets these men apart is the incredible strength in their beliefs which have given them the will power to fight on, against the incredible odds, and yet prevail. Beliefs are assumptions that empower ordinary people to do extraordinary things many think impossible. Conversely, limiting beliefs are also what keep many people from achieving what they want in life.

Your belief system is like an operating system such as Linux or Windows that helps to run your day-to-day activities. What you believe in will define what you will DO, and what you WILL ACHIEVE. I remember the day when I started my first job in a call centre. Although I was to support users for a residential broadband, I must confess that I did not know a single thing at that time.

On the first day of training, twelve of us, including the new managers, were grouped together and briefed about DSLAMPS and ADSL technology. During the course, I discovered that the managers' level of knowledge was not that much different from mine. They did not know ADSL technology better than I did. But how was it that they were they able to become managers?

After some close observation and analysis, I drew certain conclusions. Soon, I started emulating the managers' actions and behaviours. I subscribed to their values, what they believed in and understood their decision-making processes. I started acting like a manager, taking on further responsibilities on my own initiative and going the extra mile, beyond my peers to prove my capabilities. In my belief system, I had already become a manager. As a result, after a mere seven months, I was promoted to a managerial position.

If you believe in your abilities, you will become what you believe yourself possible to be. If you believe you will become a manager, a CEO, a millionaire or a president, you are one step closer to achieving your dreams. You can raise the bar, set the benchmark and exceed all expectations. Likewise, if you believe that you will fail, you already have. I once read that a circus performer who regularly does death-defying stunts like jumping from one trapeze to another started dreaming that he would one day fall off while attempting a jump. He started having these dreams regularly. Three months later, his nightmares became a reality and he fell to his death. In short, his dreams started reinforcing his belief system, resulting in terrible consequences.

If you believe that you can be a leader, then you will do what you think good leaders do from the references and experiences that you have accumulated. If your definition of a "good leader" means screaming at the top of your voice for someone to carry out a certain action, then that is what you will do when you assume a leadership position. If you define leadership to be someone respectful of others and who exhibits role model behavior, then you will translate their definitions into concrete actions upon successful assumption of position. Your belief system determines WHAT you DO and HOW you will ACT.

If you believe something is possible, you will do everything you can to make it happen. You will take massive action and diligently work towards achieving what you believe is possible. Subsequently, when you finally achieve it, it will reinforce your belief system that the very core values and rules that you believed in are true. And when you embark on your next project that you believe in, you will take similar actions that have proven useful previously. If, along the way, you meet with challenges and obstacles that threaten to derail you on your path to success, your belief system will enable you to convert any failures into lessons to be learnt, negative feedback into constructive criticism. You will be empowered to turn lemons into lemonade until you get the results that you want.

Your past successful experiences allow you to construct a set of values that you hold dear to and your future actions will be aligned to this set of values. That is the main reason why some people that subscribe to beliefs that limit them, keep failing to achieve their goals in their lives, such as achieving their ideal weight or finding Mr. Right.

After failing a couple of times, their experiences reinforce their belief systems and ultimately, no matter what they do, they will never achieve their targets or goals. Fortunately, there are ways in which we can disempower these limiting beliefs and set new and powerful core values and belief systems to empower ourselves to achieve our goals.

When two people sit together on the mountain with a view of the seaside, one may see the picturesque sunset and savour the calmness of his surroundings. On the other hand, the other may offer a totally different perspective of what he secs. In his mind may be skyscrapers of mammoth proportions, flyovers that stretch beyond the human eye and concrete results of rapid developments and technology.

This is why Steven Spielberg, one of the greatest film makers of our time, is so successful. He is an individual who is able to visualize what others cannot. He can imagine himself in a realm that has not even existed yet. He is able to specifically state what he wants done to the minute detail. In short, he has a crystal clear picture of what he wants to achieve and not just some blurry image. His desire to make movies was so strong that during a visit to the Hollywood theatre in his college years, he sneaked past the guards to catch a glimpse of how the directors worked. Needless to say, he derived his inspiration there. During the peak of his career, he made movies that stretched our imagination and awed us, using the technology which was unheard of to the layman.

Why is it that literally even from the same angle, two people may have different perspectives of the same object with a different view, differing perspective? The answer is because each of us has a different perspective of what may be true for us. Ask different people to define the idea of being rich. The replies you may get may range from being able to put three square meals on a table each day to owning two airports and a small island.

People's beliefs, based on what they have gone through, have helped shape their perspectives on every single dimension. When your belief limits you, look out for information elsewhere, where people have done what you aspire to do, and strengthen your beliefs by telling yourself you can accomplish what others have.

Even if you have set out to accomplish what nobody has done before, worry not. Roger Bannister did not wait for someone to run a mile under four minutes before he set that as his target! The key here is proper planning and execution.

Once you are absolutely clear about what you want to achieve, draw up a detailed plan on how you are going to accomplish it. My definition of "detailed" means, to be absolutely clear on the How, Where, When, What and so forth. Not just some blurry images of what desires you have over bedtime. Do also periodically review your plan until you get what you want.

How To Tap Into Your Potential

When you believe that something is possible, you will start to think of methods to transform your beliefs into reality. You will use all the resources you possess, maximize your creativity, channel all your power to achieve what you aim to achieve. Does that mean that you will be able to achieve 100% of what you want with this belief system? Far from it! In fact, you would probably fail a few times before you actually get what you want. Think of it this way, each time you fail, you are a step closer to achieving what you want. I am sure you have heard of a Chinese saying that failure is the mother of success. Thomas Edison failed countless times before actually finally creating a stable light bulb. If he had given up after a few attempts, our world would probably be still in darkness.

Most people would read with envy the names on the annual billionaire or millionaire lists in the *Forbes*. Some would wonder how these people came to be one of the

> *"It doesn't matter who you are or where you come from. The ability to triumph begins with you."*
>
> *– Oprah Winfrey –*

richest people in the world. Some would even dream to be just like them. Dreams with no plans for action will just remain as they are just dreams.

Here is a story of a woman who defied all odds, including sexual abuse to triumph against all adversities to become one of the most powerful women in the world. Her name is Oprah Winfrey. After suffering from abuse and molestation, she ran away and was sent to a juvenile detention home at the tender age of 13. Unfortunately, she was refused entry because there were no more beds available. She was later sent to live with her strict disciplinarian father, Vernon Winfrey.

At the age of 17, she embarked on a broadcasting career. After several years of hosting her own show, she formed her own production company and in 1991, motivated in part by the memories of her unfortunate childhood, initiated a campaign to establish a national database of convicted child abusers. Why would someone whom, after suffering a traumatizing childhood, be able to use that memory and that experience to create a greater good for mankind. How was it that she was able to serve the community so that others would not suffer the same fate as she did?

The difference here is that Oprah Winfrey made good use of her unpleasant experiences and believed that they were lessons others could learn from. She made sure that her suffering was not in vain. She enforced those affirmations in the best way possible to help her achieve her goals and made her lifelong aim to help others achieve and fulfill their dreams as well.

Like I had written earlier on, you should not allow a bad experience early in your life to taint you for life. Conversely, we can learn from it and develop greater strength in the face of adversity. It is interesting to note that more often than not, we learn more from our past failures than that of our past successes and glories.

The first self-development book I read that impacted me deeply was Anthony Robbins' *Awaken the Giant Within*. After reading that book, I started setting goals that had previously seemed impossible to attain. I bought more and more self-help books and started to digest and apply what I had read and learned. Furthermore, I began doing more and more research in this arena. That was when I developed to have the urge, passion and interest to share my knowledge of the potential and the possibility of what the human brain can achieve. And mind you, I am not someone who loves to read.

The reason books like these are so important is the fact that most people, in their entire lifetimes, may not have the opportunity to understand first-hand the experiences of people in different cultures, different countries, different belief systems and different lifestyles. Why is it that suicide bombers can actually convince themselves to carry out such tasks? Why do they blow themselves up and kill thousands of innocent people? It is because they are brainwashed and have a limited belief system which reinforces that their actions are correct and honorable.

Most of us are limited by personal constraints, by our own limiting beliefs and therefore develop similar traits and evolve into the people around us, like our friends and relatives. Birds of a feather flock together. Therefore, we only achieve as much or maybe a little bit more than what our parents, our peers or our colleagues have achieved. However, thanks to globalization and technology, mind-boggling possibilities are only a click away.

Have you ever heard of the Rosenthal or Pygmalion effect? Or more commonly the Teacher-Expectancy Effect whereby students performed better than others simply because they were expected to do so. In their study, Robert Rosenthal and Lenore Jacobson observed that if teachers were led to believe in the enhanced performance of their students, then those particular students would indeed show marked improvement as expected.

Let's try a little experiment. Divide children into two groups. We will name the first group the Genius Group and the second, the Average Group. In actual fact, the so-named Genius Group could consist of the mediocre learners and performers and vice versa. Next, inform the teacher who would be teaching them over the course of the semester of the two groups' labels.

At the end of the semester, the results will surprise you. It is highly possible that the results of the actual mediocre group would have improved tremendously. This is because the teacher had been led to believe that that the mediocre group was made up of intelligent students and hence would tailor his/her lessons and peg them according to the perceived the level of intelligence of the group of children.

Catering to the higher expectations of results, the teacher would have handed out many exercises and those of a higher standard to maximize the perceived capabilities of the children. The children, being exposed to these higher-order work daily would as a result develop and improve in terms of their capabilities. At the end of the day, hence their academic results would definitely improve as well. This is why parents who dubbed their children as "slow learners" or "stupid" often find that because of the Pygmalion effect, their prophecy becomes self-fulfilling. Maybe the next time you itch to call your children "stupid", you might want to hold your tongue!

Now that you realize how your belief systems can shape your perceptions and what you believe to be the truth may not be entirely true, it is time for you to decide on what you CAN do and HOW you are going to act upon that decision.

You must be also aware that your belief system can affect your emotions.

Imagine this scenario:

Every Monday morning, when you wake up, do you dread going to work, seeing your dreadful boss and imagine the tons of work piling up on your desk? Do you struggle to get out of bed, putting your alarm clock on snooze until the very last minute when you know you have to get up or you are going to be late. You should change your belief system now!

Imagine this scenario:

Come Monday morning, when you wake up, before you brush your teeth and have your breakfast, tell yourself, "It is going to be a GREAT week ahead!" Reinforce this statement at least 10 times before you leave the house and start the day. Tell yourself that your colleagues cannot wait to have you in the office, your boss thinks you are doing an amazing job and that work that day is going to be a breeze. Now reinforce this at least 10 times out loud and also in your mind. But note that you have got to believe in what you are telling yourself before your brain can actually program this into your sub-consciousness. Very soon, you will notice the difference in how you feel when you have a positive belief system as compared to previously.

Do you know that your subconscious mind will program and believe whatever you tell it to program? How many times have you had a nightmare that woke you in the middle of the night, leaving you perspiring profusely and your heart rate increased? This is because the dream had seemed so real for you. When I get nightmares like these, I will go back to sleep forcing myself to CREATE an ending in my dream that I DESIRE. Surprised? Try it! The nightmares may not be so frightening after all.

I once read an article on the very interesting topic of hypnosis. It described a human test subject who was hypnotized. An ice cube was then gently placed on the person's forearm. The test subject, who was still in a state of hypnosis, was then told that the object on his arm was a burning steel rod. Guess what happened? That person's forearm started developing blisters as if it was being scalded by a hot iron rod! The powers of the human mind!

Visualization

In the belief system, before you are able to achieve anything that you desire, you have to be able to see the end result in your mind. You must visualize what you want to achieve before you can actually achieve it. Imagine a situation with a shooter. If you blindfold him and instruct him to visualize NOT hitting the target, do you think he would be able to hit the target even though the target is only 10 metres away? Unlikely.

In the Olympics, gold medalists and silver medalists may have a mere difference of 0.01 seconds apart. More often than not, the difference is that the gold medalist is often able to visualize crossing the finishing line first before doing so. I used to play ping pong during my school days. For those of you who do not know what ping pong is, it is also known as table tennis whereby two players or four players (doubles) will hit a ball across a table separated by a mini net. It is much like tennis being played on a table.

After I started working, I did not play ping pong for about a year and a half as there were no facilities in my office nor had I the time. However, I had often visualized playing ping pong with my ex-course mates and my schoolmates in my mind. On and off, when I returned to my hometown and had the opportunity to play against them, they would ask me the same question again and again, "how many times do you practise in a week?" When I tell them that I have not played for over a year, their faces register surprise and they comment that I still display the basic moves and the agility. The answer to this phenomenon lies in the power of visualization.

Negative Belief Systems

As much as I would like to emphasize on positive belief systems, I will also need to cover negative belief systems. We must constantly be aware that it exists in all of us, whether old or young, intelligent or otherwise. How does one develop a negative belief system? Earlier on, I mentioned that most of us are surrounded by the people who are dear to us and whom we look up to, like our parents, grandparents, brothers and sisters, teachers, friends and, bosses. These people play significant roles in our lives.

We tend to follow whatever they do, and our belief systems are shaped by theirs as well. They are like mentors to us. So if these people have negative belief systems, you are likely to have some of these traits as well. For example, if they regard smoking as being "cool" and "hip" and see taking drugs as being acceptable, you will come to accept their points of view as well. Likewise, if your parents used to cane or beat you when you were young for even the slightest mistake, when you grow up and have children of you own, you are likely to do the same unless you change your belief system. This is because you were brought up to believe that whenever a mistake is made, one should be accept corporal punishment. Most of our belief systems come from our past experiences as they reinforces our belief that what we subscribe to is right.

When I was 16, I entered into the Science stream in school and Physics was a subject which I dreaded. The teacher who taught that subject was a freshie, just out of college and did not have ample experience in teaching to help me to understand the difficult concepts. In my first term, I failed miserably. No matter how hard I tried to study, I just could not improve. I started to have the belief that I was bad and lousy at that subject and with a freshie teacher who had no experience, there was no way I was going to pass my *Sijil Penilaian Menengah* (SPM). In the end, I got a D (A is for distinction, while E is the worst grade) in that subject. Each time I failed Physics, my belief system was reinforced that I was lousy and would never pass that subject, hence I failed.

Now let me share another incident. In the same year when I had Physics as one of my academic subjects, I also had Chemistry, a subject in which I would learn how different chemicals reacted. I was no better in this subject than Physics and had already decided to drop both Chemistry and Physics in the SPM (we had 9 subjects altogether). My first term exam result for Chemistry was 14 out of 100 and my highest mark was 24%!

One day, as I was sitting in the library I decided to read one of the reference books for Chemistry. I read one of the sub topics that I could not understand before. To my surprise, my understanding for that sub topic that day was crystal clear. I started reading and reading from one topic to another and found that Chemistry was much easier than I had thought. I decided to study that subject and aimed for a distinction. That was approximately 6 weeks before the finals. I managed to score a B+ in my finals. Although I did not get an A, my point here is that I had managed to subconsciously change my belief system about not being able to master the subject well enough to pass.

Now let's question ourselves. Do you have any negative belief system that you may not be aware of? When something goes wrong, do you tend to put the blame on others? Do you listen or do you judge? Do you criticize or provide? Are you part of the solution or part of the problem?

Take all the time you need to answer the above questions and then list down all the negative belief systems that you may have in certain aspects of your life.

Negative Belief System In A Relationship

Do you have a belief system that women are materialistic and only go for your wealth? Or men are wolves who prey on helpless women? Have you ever been hurt in a relationship and vowed never to trust the opposite sex again? Cameron Diaz vowed that she would never wed another actor because she believed all marriages between actors and actresses will end up in divorce.

Negative Belief System In Yourself

Do you believe that you are too old? Too young to get married? Too young to have children? Do you believe that you are lazy? Or procrastinate? Do you believe you are not smart enough? I used to believe that I would never start writing this book.

Negative Belief System In Wealth

Do you believe that rich people inherit their parents wealth automatically? Do you believe it is impossible to earn more than 5k in a month? 10k? Or maybe 100k? Do you believe that you will never be rich?

Now that you have listed down all your negative belief systems and they are currently occupying your subconscious mind, it is time to change those disempowering beliefs and turn them into empowering ones.

Empowering and Creating
Positive Belief Systems

1. **Find the reason to change your negative believe system to a positive one from a mere want to a NEED and a MUST.**

In the section above, you have listed down all the negative belief systems that you think you have. Now, what I need you to do is to select the top 20% of that belief systems.

Let's get started. Every year, on the first of January, most people make their yearly resolutions to go to the gym, to quit smoking, to find a life partner, to stop procrastinating, to make more money, to be more hardworking and the list goes on and on and on. But by the second or the third week of the month, they fall back on their old habits; getting that chocolate bar at the 7-11 counter, smoking a full pack of cigarettes instead of half a pack a month and so on. Do you have the same experience?

Most people do not change or cannot sustain the change they attempt to make because they do not give themselves strong enough reasons to do so. They tell themselves, tomorrow is the day I am going to quit smoking, and when tomorrow comes, they will tell themselves the same thing again. To change your limiting beliefs, you must give yourself enough strong fundamental reasons to change.

I have a close friend who was seven months pregnant. Her husband was a chain smoker who smoked one and a half packs of cigarettes everyday. He tried to quit several times but his attempts were always unsuccessful. He tried nicotine patches, going to counselling, and even giving his wife more money every month so that he would have less money to buy cigarettes. Nothing worked. His addiction kept coming back.

From 10 sticks a day and slowly half a pack to one and a half packs. Her husband loved her dearly and they were expecting their first child after their previous miscarriage. One day, there was a big argument about her nagging him to stop smoking as she feared her child would be affected by it. Seeing that she still could not talk him into quitting smoking, she gave him an ultimatum. "Quit smoking or I will divorce you!" At that time she was eight and a half months pregnant and was ready to deliver.

When their baby boy was born, her husband visited her in the hospital when they were still having their "cold war". When he set eyes on his son, he told me that he had seen the most wonderful thing in the world and that this child was the most wonderful and amazing thing that had ever happened to him. At that moment, he told his wife, he would quit smoking. And voila, just like that, he quit smoking. He did not suffer from any more addictions or any syndromes that would trap him into smoking again. Even when he went out for meals with his smoker friends, he was never tempted to light another cigarette again.

As illustrated, when you turn your belief system into a WANT and MUST SUCCEED, you CAN DO IT too. My friend's husband managed to turn his negative belief system of not able to quit smoking after so many failed attempts into a positive and reinforcing one because he believes that the love of his life, his wife, and his new born baby were worth every effort, no matter how difficult it was going to be. He knew he HAD to quit. He knew he MUST. He gave himself no other choice but to succeed. And succeed he did.

When you do not allow yourself to fail and give yourself enough reasons to succeed, there is no other path but success. It is the same concept with any other achievements in your life. If you want to lose weight but have not enough courage or determination to start, give yourself an ultimatum, tell your closest friend or the people that look up to you and announce to them that you want to start losing weight and start going to the gym again. Challenge yourself in front of all your closest allies. That way, you put your own reputation on the line. When you fail, you lose your reputation. You give yourself NO OTHER CHOICE BUT TO SUCCEED.

2. **On your negative belief system list, note down all the evidence or past experience that made you believe that this belief is true. How did you reinforce that negative experience over the years to make it one of your belief systems? How did you find that this belief system is "true"?**

For instance, I mentioned earlier that I did not excel in Physics. This negative system was further reinforced by me failing the subject each term and by the teacher whom I perceived to be without any credible experience in making weak students like me understand the concepts and therefore improve.

Next, challenge your belief system. Look at the other side of the coin. From another perspective, look at your situation from a different light. Did I fail because I was using the wrong method of study? Did I fail to understand the concepts that were relayed to me by the teacher because I had asked the wrong questions? How do I change my methods of study into more effective ones? Interactive discussions with my fellow peers? Going for additional tuition classes? Doing more exercises rather than just memorizing all the facts and regurgitating them, perhaps? I applied all these new methods for Chemistry which I also dreaded and planned to fail! When I looked back, it was so obvious and evident that I could have applied the same concepts on Physics but did not.

Stop asking questions like why the teacher keeps teaching something that I cannot understand or why I keep failing. Do not question whether it is because I am slow. When you ask yourself these questions, the answers will inevitably lead to answers like because the teacher is new or has no experience (something that is beyond your control), I keep failing because I am stupid (which is another reinforcement of a negative belief system).

By asking the correct questions like HOW can I improve further? What more CAN I do? When can I achieve my goals? How can I challenge these limiting beliefs into new empowering beliefs? What other methods are possible? Who else has done it before? Get information from reliable sources whom you can trust to reinforce your positive belief system. Remember, always focus on what you CAN DO and what you CAN CONTROL. You can control yourself. You can DO what you THINK you can. Asking the correct questions will get you new and powerful answers.

3. **Once you have found enough reasons to justify why you NEED and MUST change your current NEGATIVE belief systems, the next step for you is to find a new empowering belief system to replace the old. Once you have cast enough doubts on your old negative belief system, it is time to develop a new empowering belief systems.**

    Create enough supporting evidence until you are 100% sure that you TOO can change. If your belief system is that you are old and there is not much time left, search for people who have gained famed or succeeded only when they are your age or older. Lillian Too, the famous *feng shui* master, did not become famous until much later in her life. Nelson Mandela became the President of South Africa when he was 76-years-old, after being imprisoned for 27 years. Those long years in prison did not stop him. Hardships and setbacks should not stop you either.

    If you belief that you are overweight and can never lose weight, then search for people who have succeeded in losing weight and are living healthily now. But know that there is truth in the saying that Rome wasn't built in a day. It takes consistent action on your part to change. Success is the result of consistently taking action with proper planning. If you have no target, no game plan, you may be motivated to lose weight, to earn money, to learn how to drive for one week or so. After that, most probably you will lose your drive and go back to your normal routine.

For each new empowering belief system, list down at least 10 (more if you want to) supporting evidence where by you know it has worked before, whether from people around you or elsewhere in the world. If you have got no sufficient examples or evidence, then make it up. Keep telling yourself this everyday and soon you will realize that the evidence you have made up is actually feasible and useful. You will not be able to tell the difference between whether it is real or not. Think about it, why are some people afraid of the dark? It is because when darkness falls, their belief system makes up enough evidence that maybe something bad will happen and this belief plays in their mind over and over again until they believe it is true. You can do the same, but in a POSITIVE way!

4. **After you have set up your new belief system and are comfortable with it, I would like you to reflect on how you would have behaved differently to a situation that has happened to you recently. You need to be aware how differently this new belief system is going to affect your future and where it will take you. And believe**

me, this new belief system will change your life and take you to places.

Then, visualize yourself in a situation where you will use your belief system to tackle and make decisions. For instance, if you feel your boss is always giving you extra work, use your new belief system and ask what this could mean. Is it because he is preparing you for the next position available? Or is it because he values your talent and knows that only you can get the job done?

Remember, we are what we think. With our thoughts we can shape our world.

II
BE MOTIVATED!
FEEL INSPIRED!

> "Motivation is what
> gets you started,
> habit is what keeps
> you going"
> – Anonymous –

The phrase "Is it a bird? Is it a plane? No, it is Superman!" was popularized with the release of the movie *Superman* in 1978, which took the movie world by storm and catapulted Christopher Reeves to fame.

As a child, Reeves was an extraordinary individual who excelled and had many talents. He had many interests, an uncanny ability to take risks, and rose to challenges. Right from the very beginning he knew what he wanted, he knew where he belonged and he worked hard to make sure that he reached his goals. He never once doubted that he belonged in the theatres.

At the age of 14, one of the directors working with Reeves told him, "You had better decide what you want, because you are going to get it". What a powerful, yet simple message to him. It had stuck with him ever since. Once we have decided what we want, when our mind allows it to happen, when there is no doubt that we are able to achieve what we set out to do, we can be damn sure that there is only one outcome at stake: we are going to get what we want.

After acting in a few more *Superman* sequels, Reeves became widely known by the public as Superman. In May 1995, Reeves was severely paralyzed in a horse riding incident that limited his movement from the neck down. His wife, Dana Reeves, stood by him and offered the support he needed to hurdle his paralysis. It was then that the real superman emerged. Reeves went on to raise awareness on spinal cord injury and stem cell research. He went on to speak at many engagements about motivation relating to disability issues. He even had a small role in a movie and directed another called *In the Gloaming.*

Bishop Jonathan D. Keaton aptly described Reeves as the real Superman. He has been widely regarded by people as Superman because he found the strength in his incapacity to use his tragedy to help others facing this life-challenging role. He kept hope alive in the face of injury and paralysis which can destroy all hopes. He remained committed to his role as a loving husband and a doting father. Christopher Reeves was SUPERMAN. He was a leader. He was an inspiration. He let us see what many of us thought impossible. He moved mountains.

I believe that there is a Superman in all of us. Granted, we may not be able to lift a crane with one hand, nor fly from one place to another, nor cut through metal rods with laser beams coming from our eyes. What I mean by Superman is that, each of us has the desire and the capability to do more than what our present condition allows us. We are able to strive for more and improve ourselves to be better, to inspire and motivate others and to help those that are weaker than us. What your mind is able to conceive, it can achieve.

It is ironic to say that when I started writing this chapter, motivation and inspiration related, I was not at my best. I was having issues juggling my time at work: the workload was piling up every day; my productivity plummeted and my health nosedived to the point that I had to be given injections for gastric problems twice in a period of six weeks due to the stress levels. At home, my love life was a mess and all my friends around me seemed to be going places, except me. Needless to say, my self-esteem was nil.

When I was on medical leave because of the gastro-enteritis, I took a few days off to recover from the medical ailment as well as psychologically. In the first couple of days, I spent about 20 hours each day in bed, doing a little bit of reading and only getting up when it was absolutely necessary. On the second day, I started thinking, "How long am I going to feel like this?", "How long am I going to feel sorry for myself?" I forced myself out of bed, turned on the computer, started clearing my mail and researching for this chapter. I would be the biggest hypocrite for trying to write an article about motivation and inspiration when I could not even get motivated myself. Who would even bother to read, let alone feel inspired? At that particular moment, I began feeling more and more motivated and all the materials and ideas began pouring in. I took a hot bath, and headed straight to the gym. YES, you heard me correctly, the GYM! From a guy who could not get himself up a few hours ago, I was now doing chin ups and bench presses at the gym.

I am sharing this experience not to brag but to say that it is not what happens to you that matters, but how you handle what happens that makes the difference. How you define what happens to you will decide whether you have what it takes to overcome it. I changed the way I defined the situations that happened to me regarding my work, my medical condition, my personal life. I took out a piece of paper and scribbled the situations that I was in, and the possible solutions to those situations, and then committed myself to start acting on those solutions.

I decided not to focus on the negative experiences that I had had but to learn from them so that I can be a better person, a stronger me. YES, a stronger me! If I kept focusing on the negative side, I would probably still be in bed! In our conscious mind, there are millions of pieces of information being processed by our brain each day. While we may not realize this, our brain selectively filters this information and allows us to focus on certain bits of information at a given time.

Similarly, when we think of an experience from the past or think about something in the future, we tend to focus on certain aspects of that particular experience, regardless of whether it is good or bad. For instance, if two people watch the movie *Spiderman*, one person may focus on the fighting scenes between Spiderman and the Green Goblin, while the other may focus on the romantic scenes between Mary Jane and Peter Parker. When you ask both people what the movie was all about, you will definitely get two different answers. Mind you, both answers are correct! It is the same with our day-to-day life: some people have a tendency to focus on negative experiences and repeating them over and over again in their minds, which will put them in an unresourceful state, while other people have the tendency to focus on the positive advantages of each situation, and put themselves in a resourceful state. Because we do this on a daily basis and unconsciously, many of us are not aware of the detrimental effects on our mental state and our overall being when we focus on the negative aspects of an experience.

I have a close friend who had just broken up with her boyfriend of seven years. When I met up with her, she looked awful, depressed and suicidal. She kept on thinking about the negative experience of the break-up and how miserable she felt at that time and how she deserved to be alone; you name it, whatever negative emotions you can think of, she had them. I told her instead of focusing on the negative aspects of the break up, to focus on the seven wonderful years that she had with him; focus on the good times, the memories that no one, and I mean it, NO ONE except herself, can take away. She looked at me with a puzzled expression. A week later, she called me up and thanked me for what I had said that day. You decide what you want to focus on. You decide how you want to frame a certain experience that you have just had. Nobody else does but YOU. REMEMBER THAT!

Is Motivation Permanent?

Have you ever felt as though you are on top of the world? That you can take on any given challenge the world throws at you? That nothing in this world can take you out of your stride? Sure you have! Everybody has. Perhaps you have just had the most wonderful weekend in your life. Perhaps your girlfriend has just accepted your marriage proposal. Maybe you have just got a raise or a promotion. Maybe nothing happened! You just decided to feel that way! Now the most glaringly obvious question is why wouldn't I want to feel this way all the time? Surely I will be more productive, I can think better and all my problems can be easily solved! And the good news is you can feel motivated all the time. Anytime at all! And YES, motivation can be permanent if YOU allow it to be.

However, I would not hide the fact that sometimes we wake up in the morning feeling miserable for something awful we did the previous night, or with the feeling of dread of what is to come later in the day. All sorts of emotions start to fill us over before the day has even begun and by the time we head out for the office, we feel as if everyone is against us or nothing of what we do seems right. Yes, even I get this feeling once in a while as illustrated by my previous experience. It happens to the best of us. It is up to you, nonetheless, to decide how you want to feel that particular moment, be it happy, excited, nervous, weird, awkward and so forth. It is of vital importance that when you are feeling down, you acknowledge and are aware that you do not feel 100% today and may not be able to leap from one building to another! Like what my mum used to tell me, "When you know where you are, you can get to where you want to go". Likewise, when you know you are feeling uneasy or down, you can turn that situation around and make yourself feel better. In the following sections, I will show you how to make motivation permanent and yes, how to motivate yourself and others.

What Is Motivation?

Before we can even start to motivate ourselves, let alone others, we need to understand what motivation is and how it works. To put it plainly, motivation is a drive from within, a voice if you will, be it your own or others', that prompts you or others to act on certain tasks and responsibilities. It is a force that determines and enables people to act in certain ways to satisfy their needs and others'. Different types of motivation will impact our lives differently. If you use the wrong type of motivational style, chances are, you are only doing what is absolutely necessary just to get by instead of living life to its fullest potential.

When was the last time you felt absolutely motivated to do something? Be it for yourself, or for others. It can be a daily chore or a goal that you had planned months in advance. What motivated you to take out the garbage? What motivated you to pick up your phone and call your friend? If your office hours are Monday to Friday, why is it that each Friday, you feel fantastic no matter what happens in the office?

Well, there could be millions of answers to questions like these. First of all, you picked up the garbage because you knew it was necessary. You picked it up because you knew if you did not, your house would stink. You picked up the phone and called your friend because you were motivated by the potential of what the conversation could bring. You made that call because you were excited by the prospect of discussing something with your friend, a date, or perhaps an assignment. Now if you are working office hours, you are motivated on a Friday, more so when it is almost time to leave for the weekend, because you know when you punch out, you do not have to worry about anything else related to work for the next two days. You know you will be out partying hard that weekend. And you know you do not have your boss breathing down your neck each time you make a terrible decision.

Now make no mistake, we could feel this way all day long. I want you to take some time to think of the occasions when you have felt down, miserable or in short, de-motivated. It could have been on a Sunday night, when you knew that when you woke up in the morning the next day, it would be a long week ahead. It could have been a meeting with your supervisor for an appraisal which you knew you would never get. You could have been turned down for a date, a promotion, or gotten embarrassed by your friends or peers. When any of these events occurred, how did you respond? That is right, you responded with a negative emotion that caused you to feel worried, de-motivated, angry, helpless, and so on and so forth.

If you dread going to work on a Monday morning and feeling the Monday blues, I want you to write down five reasons why you should be feeling good! For starters, you should be thankful that you still have a job, you could be thankful that you will be meeting your colleagues, some of whom have already been your best friends for a number of years. You can also be thankful that you have a boss that you may like. You may also want to be grateful that there are millions of others who crave jobs that you currently have, people that would decide in a heartbeat, "Hey! I would do whatever it took to be in that man's position!"

If you are feeling dreadful and are convinced that your appraisal with your supervisor will not be a successful one, similar to the X number of times previously tried, challenge yourself and your supervisor to why things should be different this time around. Similarly, give yourself 5 reasons why you think the appraisal should be a positive one. Justify it with supporting facts, documents and statistics to prove that you deserve the raise. If you cannot find 5 reasons, perhaps you may want to change the way you work or increase your productivity. Yet again, the key here is to identify that you, YES YOU, have what it takes to feel motivated regardless of the situation. It is how you respond to that situation that makes the difference.

Likewise, if you are getting turned down for a promotion, a date or request, respond to it positively. Identify five possible reasons why it happened, and tell yourself why you will nail it the next time. Again, give yourself five ways in which you will absolutely feel better prepared next time when a similar opportunity knocks on your door. Yes, how you respond to that situation will determine whether you feel bad or de-motivated.

There is a company where my good friend worked, which was doing some restructuring and therefore downsizing. Retrenchment rate was rather high at that time. One interesting thing is, as much as they wanted to downsize, they had to find people to fill up positions at the top. So they passed out some small red envelopes, with news of whether you were promoted or retrenched. My friend found this envelope on his table when he came into the office one day.

Before opening it, he expressed disappointment and kept saying how much he had contributed to the company and should not be retrenched. All day long he was browsing through websites, looking for new job openings and scheduling the next month for interviews. He also started making phone calls to his previous companies to see if they had any openings for him. Additionally, he started planning where to cut down on his budget for the next month. He did ALL THAT, before opening the envelope. When he got home, he opened the envelope to see how much back pay the company still owed him and when his last serving day was in the office. To his utter disbelief, the envelope was for a promotion the company had offered him, to Assistant Vice President. Just imagine what could have happened had he not opened the envelope and continued looking for a new job!

All these feelings of positiveness and negativity are illustrated in a very interesting concept of:

Event + Response = Outcome

This concept illustrates that an event or an experience that happens to you, whether directly or indirectly, plus whatever response that you define the event to be, whether you choose to respond to it positively or otherwise, will determine the outcome of that experience. This is true to some extent.

Take this scenario for instance:

You are someone who enjoys attention and your birthday is a very important occasion for you. Your birthday comes, your best friend, or more importantly, your loved one, does not call or buy you any gift. What would be your reaction? Or more importantly, what would be your response? Would you assume that your best friend has forgotten about your birthday? Or maybe your loved one does not care much to celebrate your birthday with you?

Make no mistake, how you react or respond towards such situation is based on your assumptions of why your best friend or loved one has failed to celebrate your birthday with you. If your assumption is a positive one, so will your response be. Likewise, if your reaction is a negative one, I can bet that your response will be a poor one. Therefore, before we can confirm any situation at all, no matter how hopeless or how dire, it is best to think positively to avoid making a wrong assumption and the situation worse. Which one is better? To be positive, to be confident about the assumption that you are making and find out at the end that it is a correct assumption, OR to be negative, blaming yourself and others about the assumption that you are making and to find out at the end what you assumed is proven to be correct?

Logically speaking, both end results are the same. But believe me, from the start of your assumption until the end, if it is a negative assumption, it would have affected your emotions and even your ability to think logically. Hence your productivity would definitely be affected, as illustrated earlier by the example with the red envelopes.

What Is Inspiration?

It is not often that you hear news which bring you close to tears. It is even rarer to hear of people sacrificing their own

37

interests and time to raise awareness for something of a greater cause for the entire community of people living in this world.

Terry Fox was born in Manitoba, Canada and raised in Port Coquitlam, British Columbia, a community near Vancouver in Canada. He was an active teenager who loved sports. At the age of 18, Fox was diagnosed with a type of bone cancer. As a result, he had to have his leg amputated six inches above his knee.

While he was in the hospital, he was moved by the suffering of other cancer patients, many of them children younger than himself. Thus he decided to run across Canada to raise money for cancer research. He called his run the marathon of hope. He kept this plan a secret from his family. For 18 months he trained and trained, telling his family that he was running to join a marathon. As he was about to start his run, he announced his plan to his family. He told them that his dream was to collect $1 from everyone in the country. At the time, Canada had a population of 24 million.

After running for about five months, covering over 5,000 kilometres (roughly about 42 kilometres daily), he was forced to stop running because his cancer had spread to his lungs. Terry Fox passed away after several months in the hospital. His legacy was just about to begin. During that duration, he managed to raise $24.17 million, surpassing his initial target.

His mum said that Terry Fox was just an ordinary young man. Well this "ordinary young man" had a heart of gold. To many Canadians, he became a national hero when he ran across the country to raise money for cancer research, all the more so when he himself was a cancer sufferer. He represented everything that was good, inspiring, generous, selfless and decent. He was indeed an altruist. To date, the Terry Fox foundation has managed to raise $400 million.

When you set your goals, do you want your goals to be just for the moment, or do you want them to live on after you have moved on to other goals? Or maybe after you have died? Legacy is something that you build, which will continue to move on even after you are long gone, and there are people who continue what you have started, and maybe even improve on whatever you have helped initiate. If you want that to happen you need to leave a good, lasting impression on the projects that you start. When Terry Fox started his marathon of hope, indeed all he had was the hope that one day enough money would be allocated to help cancer research.

Without hope, there is nothing humans can accomplish. With a ray of hope, no matter how impossible the task may seem, it can spur the human spirit to a greater cause many may think impossible. Hope is powerful when used with proper planning and initiated with action.

The reason I included inspiration in this chapter is because I strongly believe and know from the bottom of my heart, through experience and trial and error, that inspiration and motivation are interrelated, if not similar. Without inspiration, there can be no motivation. The two words are inseparable. But how do we deduce inspiration? Is it something tangible? Is it something we can measure? If so, how? How do I feel inspired? Before you can feel inspired, first you need to know what inspiration is.

Now according to the Oxford Dictionary, inspiration is a process, an event, a person, a song; be it tangible or not, that causes someone or a group of people to have exciting new ideas, or makes them want to create something new, something exciting, whether for themselves or for others. It is something to make people feel they want to improve for the better. It can be as simple as a powerful quote from someone whom you look up to, to something complicated like the ability to solve a difficult geometry problem.

If you are a person that gets your daily dose of inspiration from people, you will get inspired by people you look up to, people that act in accordance to the belief systems that you hold up to; people who do things that relate to what you agree with, to what you believe in. Think about it. Have you ever followed or felt inspired by someone who has the totally opposite point of view, or someone whom you despise? I doubt it.

If you go to church or Sunday class, you are probably used to hearing the pastor or the Sunday class teacher preach about lessons in life, what to do and what not to do. You probably listen to them, as they are people of influence.

Let me share this short story with you. A new pastor moved into a new neighborhood and was finding his way around the small town. He wanted to know where the post office was. While he was strolling around, he stopped and asked an 11-year-old boy, "Good evening son, would you be kind enough to show me where the post office is located?" The boy replied, "Just walk straight and you will be able to see it on the next block". The pastor thanked the boy and before he headed to the post office, asked him, "Since you showed me how to get to the post office, why don't you come to church this Sunday? I will show you the way to heaven". The boy looked at the pastor and bluntly replied, "Thanks, but I don't think I will be there. You do not even know your way to the post office".

To inspire someone, one must know what that person is motivated by. If you want to motivate yourself, you need to visualize a target to achieve, set the desired outcome, and have visual indicators along the way to monitor your progress so that you can keep track of it. Find out what inspires you to do certain things that you do. They can be events on a daily basis that make you wonder: What motivates you to go look for lunch? What inspires you to go to the gym to work out? What inspires you to go to the office on time? Respectively, it can be hunger, the desire to look good or the fear that you will lose your job should you arrive late. It is just as an archer requires a target before he can fire that arrow, you need a target before you can be motivated and inspired. And that target needs to be empowering, a target that you are passionate about; a target that you think about every single day; a target that excites you; a target that gives you the reason to wake up with enthusiasm every single morning! Yes, those kinds of targets!

Journey To The Destination

The trip to our designated target is seldom a straight road without any difficulties. There will come a time when we are faced with the daunting trip that we feel is taking its toll on us, whether emotionally or physically. There are times when we feel the whole world is against us. When we feel de-motivated, we are at a loss for inspiration and want to just give up and let the current take us. At times like these, motivation and things that inspire us are key to getting us back on track again. In fact, it is how we RESPOND POSITIVELY to situations, instead of reacting negatively, that determines whether we will achieve our desired outcome.

This is why effective motivation techniques are so essential because they enable you to use what is fresh on your mind, and use what you have been taught through your various life experiences. Do you know that when inspirational information is absorbed into the brain in an enthusiastic way, it causes the brain to release neurotransmitters that enhance the way you think, rejuvenate your body, energize your being and increase your creativity? If you have been to a motivational talk, did you notice that each time after the seminar or the presentation, your brain sets off in motion a number of creative ideas, thoughts and preferences? This is because your brain responds positively to the message delivered in the seminar and you feel inspired by the message and motivated to get things going again. Each time I get an opportunity to attend a presentation, a seminar or a talk, I get my scrap book ready because I know I will get fresh new ideas, new goals to set and achieve. Even though I have attended these seminars before, I know that they are worth my time if I can get one new idea from them each time.

In 2006, one of my closest friends was appointed Operational Divisional Manager of his company. It was quite a feat as he was only 27-years-old at the time. Most people in that position in his company were above 35 years old. There were 13 supervisors under his wing and each one was responsible to do direct selling, make business presentations, make cold calls and do a lot of other client-related work. They dealt directly with the clients and set their expectations.

Needless to say, he was on top of the world, being given such a huge responsibility at a young age. Of course, he had the know-how and the expertise that came with the job. Soon after, his fairy tale world began to collapse and problem after problem began to surface. Three of his supervisors were under official investigations for embezzlement of company funds, and one of his longest serving supervisors was involved in a nasty highway accident, and had to be hospitalized for two months. In a little more than a month, sales plummeted, employee attrition was at an all time high and there were rumors that he was too young to be promoted, and that the management had made the wrong decision.

You can imagine the amount of stress and pressure he was under. He took a five day break to go back to his hometown to prepare for his headquarters meeting cum presentation to present his case and justify the sales numbers. He went to the bus station and got a book written by Anthony Robbins, *Awaken The Giant Within* for the journey back.

After three days, he called me up and told me, "This book has just saved my career! I felt as though this book was specifically written for me". He explained further, "I am not responsible for the decisions of the three men who embezzled funds, nor am I responsible for the accident that had happened to my supervisor. However, I am responsible for how I can handle the situation, how I can pull the company out of this mini crisis, and how I can justify the plummeting sales volume with a thorough, step-by-step action plan on what needs to be done". The remaining two days were spent crafting out a specific seven-way plan to turn the business around. He spelled out what needed to be done, what were the specific goals of his covering officers and set the expectations with the remaining staff.

Take note that nothing changed out there, the three men were still under investigation (they were eventually dismissed), and his supervisor was still out with a broken leg and two broken ribs. But his way of thinking changed. His attitude changed. He turned on his creative juices, became motivated, and renewed his commitment towards the company despite the fact there were rumors that they may demote him in the upcoming meeting. He set extremely specific objectives, underlined his desire with clear and specific goals and went off to work with a renewed passion.

The rest is history! He turned the division around, increased sales by almost two fold within nine months and was voted Manager of the Year two years later. As you can see, more often than not, it is not what happens to you but how you define and handle what happens that makes the difference. It is less important where you start, but more important where you want to go, and how you make your journey there that counts most.

Sometimes when you set too big a goal, things can work against you. When the going gets tough, it is easy to just throw in the towel. If these goals are broken down into specific smaller goals or milestones, and you start achieving each milestone, celebrate it! Reward yourself with small gestures and tokens of appreciation so that you are able to motivate yourself toward achieving the ultimate goal, the ultimate objective.

Hope And Expectations

Here is another remarkable story that will strengthen and highlight the fact that properly executed, powerful and positive affirmations, can become a reality. Remember that allowing something to happen can only manifest into reality in the absence of doubt.

When Cassius Clay started his boxing career, he had some significant characteristics that he went on to display throughout his boxing career. He used to brag to everyone about his strength, swiftness and how nobody could beat him. Before each fight, he would tell his opponent and the media in which round he will knock out his rival.

Imagine the affirmation of his conviction and the confidence that this man had. He had made it absolutely necessary that in each fight, he must win no matter what, since he had announced to the world that he would beat his opponent. He knew he could not fail each time he went inside the ring. He could not disappoint his fans. Because he knew that if he had predicted wrongly, people would lose their respect for him. And more often than not, he had correctly predicted the number of rounds that his opponents would stand before being knocked out.

Here is the man who popularized the phrase, "Float like a butterfly, Sting like a bee". He was also known as GOAT – Greatest of All Time. When he boxed, he made sure he gave his best. He made sure that there was only one outcome. He made sure that when the judge called off the fight, he would be the boxer left standing. No two ways about it.

This is a man who was born in an era when war was the talk of the town, an era in which confidence was almost

> *"You lose nothing when you fight for a cause. Losers are those who fight for nothing they care about"*
>
> *– Muhammad Ali –*

non-existent. Here is a man who had motivated and inspired the entire nation, if not the whole world, to fight for peace and equality among all people in the world. He was known as Muhammad Ali after having embraced Islam.

When you want something badly, impossible is no longer a word that you will seek to understand and comprehend.

Hope is a feeling that we want something to happen and think that it is still possible, no matter how small or minute the possibility. It is a belief that deep down inside, you know something better will come about. This is what drives us to do what others may think is foolish. It is what keeps Kimi Raikonen racing on till the penultimate race of the season and hopes that his main title rivals will drop points along the way. And they do. Hope is what keeps the Liverpool team who are losing by three goals at half time to play on in the hope that they will tire the opponents and score a couple of early goals to level the score and maybe even win the game. And this they do. Hope is what keeps medical scientists continue their research on cures for diseases that have plagued mankind for centuries.

Imagine a situation where there is no hope and everything is for certain, and you know exactly what is going to happen to yourself, others and everything in your life. You know what the score of the football game is going to be. You know whether your girlfriend is going to accept your proposal. You know if you are going to get promoted.

Ultimately, you know when you are going to die. The world would come to a standstill; no one would attempt to do anything if they already knew the result. Eventually, mankind would cease to exist. Therefore, this four letter word, HOPE, carries a substantial weight in our lives.

Life is similar in many ways. When we sense and hope that something positive is going to happen, we are energized dramatically. We feel better. We are more confident no matter how small the possibility is. Likewise, when we fear that we are going to lose or fail, we are affected negatively and thus have negative results.

That is why motivation is not only important for the good times, but more so for the bad. A person who knows how to motivate himself will be more successful, achieve more and all will reflect in the final outcome.

Failure As A Motivator? Why Not!

Fear of failure is far more destructive than failure. In any area of life, fear of failure can defeat you before you even begin. Everyone, at any one time, has felt like a complete failure. While some allow the fear of failure to destroy them, others manage to overcome it and go on to become successful and conquer their fears. Which of these kinds of people are you?

What makes us afraid of failure? Are we afraid of what others may think? Or are we afraid of the consequences? Sometimes we assume that just because we have failed once, twice or even three times, we are complete failures and a disgrace to the people we love, the people that we care about. What a preposterous assumption! How many people are completely successful the first time? Very often the success stories that you read in the newspapers, of superstars and athletes, are the result of years of training, and most of all, their successes are based upon the many failures that they have endured. The most successful people are the ones who learn from their mistakes and turn their failures into stepping stones and opportunities. Every opportunity, every single invention, every business success story and every relationship has resulted in a series of failures and setbacks. No one can live without failure. Thomas Edison had failed more than 1,000 times before he found the flicker of light. He did not see the failures as mere failures but opportunities to keep pushing on, to keep trying to find the right formula. If you have failed in love, it means that you have tried, you have given your best shot and it is better to have loved and failed than never to have loved at all.

A failure means you have put some effort into the event, no matter how small, no matter how minute. It means that you have tried, or you may have been persuaded by your friend to try. That is a start. Failure means an opportunity to try again, but this time, to do it differently and to find a better way to do it. And that exudes positiveness. It teaches you something that you should have done and adds to your life experience. How many times have you sat with your good buddies over a glass of wine, reminiscing about the times you were young, how silly you were and what you would have done differently? How many times have you sat with your business associates, wondering what happened that cost you the deal? Now that is good news. As you brainstorm, this process teaches you life's lesson of avoiding similar results from occurring the next time you are faced with the same situation.

> *"Success comes from good judgment. Good judgment comes from experience, and experience, more often than not, comes from bad judgment!"*
> — Anthony Robbins —

Failure is an event, never a person, nor an attitude, nor an outcome. It is a temporary inconvenience, or even a stepping stone to greater things to come. Our response to it determines how helpful failure can be. Yesterday's failure ended last night, so do not keep harping on it. Today is a brand new day, so enjoy it; it is a gift, that is why they call it the "present". Tomorrow is an unknown blessing, thus plan for it so that you know what to expect.

Motivation For Continuous Personal Growth

I always remember the philosophy of one of the most sought after motivational speakers, Zig Ziglar, who said, "You can have everything you want in life if you will just help enough other people get what they want, to work for your benefit and the benefit of mankind". I could not agree more with this principle. If we keep working towards self-fulfillment, this thought pattern will lead to difficulty; we will hit a ceiling whereby we cannot grow anymore. Self-fulfillment restricts growth, creativity and productivity on the job. Do not get me wrong. I am not saying that striving continuously to improve yourself is not a good thing; what I am saying is that motivation for personal growth is a two-way street that benefits two parties, creates a win-win situation for both the creator and the receiver. Motivation for personal growth is like your personal tuition teacher who acquires the knowledge required to teach others who in turn improve. Have you ever heard of the saying "To teach is to learn twice"? It is the same concept: the more we strive to teach others and share with them what knowledge we have, the more in-depth knowledge we will acquire on that particular subject matter.

Before we move on to the next chapter, I cannot stress enough how essential it is to know how to be motivated in our daily lives. Regular doses of motivation and inspiration will lead to better health, happiness, achievement and fulfillment physically, mentally and spiritually. Know what can motivate you, and it will lead you on your way to a better life!

III
GOALS: YOUR
DRIVING FORCE

"I realized the commitment to do well and to be well is a lifetime of choices that you make daily. The space to live in is not 'I'll try'. Not 'I want to'. Not 'I really want to'. It's 'I have decided'."

– Oprah Winfrey –

Previously, back in the call centre where I worked, we had to deal with complaint cases on a daily basis. We had about five cases a day and a typical complaint could take 1-2 hours to follow up and close. I once had an assistant team leader, a supervisor who used to come to the office and tell everyone, "Today I'm going to get some cases done". However, at the end of each day, cases were incomplete and not tended to for a few days following, while emails were not responded. The service level was so bad that I had to take immediate action, or risk getting more complaints. So when I came to the office the following day, I asked him, "There are about

15 cases pending in your queue yet to be closed, so how many are you going to close today?" He looked at me blankly and replied "I am going to clear off a few cases today". I asked again, "How many is a few?" Slightly irritated, I gave him an ultimatum before he had the chance to respond, "You are going to clear 15 cases today. And at the end of the day, you are going to write me a report on each of the cases". Period. At the end of that day, he cleared the 15 cases and even furnished me with a report. Amazing, isn't it?

Guys, the point is this: if you close your eyes and aim your shot towards a target, how can you hit it without knowing where it is? The concept is the same with goals. To achieve anything in life, be it in your relationship with your loved ones, your career, your personal development, you must have a set of specific goals which are measurable and achievable.

In this chapter, I'm going to share with you the magic of setting empowering goals, and how you can achieve these goals in just four simple steps.

What do you want?

Sometimes, in order to do well and be ahead of others, we must do things differently. We have to realize that being different may not necessarily be a bad thing.

One of the greatest athletes of all time and a living legend, Michael Johnson, prides himself in doing things that have never been done before. He has smashed countless world records in the track and field world and remained unbeaten in his field for one whole year! That is a staggering achievement by any standard! Not only that, as of today, his 400 m record is still standing and yet to be broken.

Here is a man who ran differently, with an unusual style that many people weren't accustomed to. He defied science, and ran with a unique posture that many so called experts claimed to be unsuitable and would only slow him down. When quizzed on his unique-running style, he simply replied, "If I had run the same way like the rest of them, I would be back there with them".

When we were at school, we often wanted to be part of a crowd, a group of peers that had common interests and ideas. If we had a new and different idea which was far from the norm, it would simply be shrugged off or people would simply retort back, "but this is the way it has been done all this while". Some may have even regarded us as freaks. Over time, our confidence diminished and we ended up "just like the rest of them".

That's why it's extremely important to know clearly what you truly want. When you're specific enough to know your desires, your goals, what people think will not matter as much. The criticism that you receive is just a small hiccup compared to what you know you can achieve. You'll have the last laugh. Persevere and have the right belief system and you will be able to stay on track. And remember to never let anybody belittle your dreams because those who do, have no dreams of their own.

It's imperative that you know exactly what you want from life. What do you want to achieve? What do you want to be in one year's time? Two years'? Five? Ten? Many times it's not what you want, but what you are willing to accept that matters. A distraught wife hopes that her husband mends his philandering ways, but is willing to accept them as long as he provides food on the table, and she will stick by him. An average student hopes to get a distinction but will accept a general pass. The office executive hopes for a higher salary but is willing to accept a 10% annual increase in salary. Get the point? Are your goals and aspirations an absolute must, that you would do absolutely anything you can conjure up? Or are they merely something you desire and hope you will attain as time goes on? In the past, when you set up certain goals, were you truly committed to making absolutely sure that you achieved those goals no matter what it took? If what you want is merely a want or a dream, without any concrete plan of achieving it, a dream is what it will remain…

Raise Your Acceptance Level

If you want to achieve more than what you currently have, you need to raise the bar two or even three times higher than your previous standard. You need to set crazy stretch goals (which will be discussed in a subsequent section).

Have you ever wondered what influences our acceptance level? Why is it that one student won't accept anything but a distinction while another will gladly accept a general pass on their exam? The level of acceptance is generally influenced by parents or peers in your environment. Remember, there is absolutely nothing wrong with following norms set by parents or peers. What I'm saying is that you have control over the level of acceptance. You can change it if you will. You can be an exception and raise the bar to a level your peers haven't seen before.

I had a friend who worked as an engineer in the airline industry. Initially, when he got accepted to study engineering, every one of us was quite envious as we knew that by the time he graduated, his income would be leaps and bounds above ours. However, whenever we met him, he would complain about how miserable his life was and how lucky or fortunate some of us were, going through life the conventional way. He always said, "If only I could quit my job now and start the business I have always wanted". He also added that he wished he could be just like me, with nothing to worry about and so much freedom to do what I want. When I challenged and encouraged him to quit his job and pursue his dream, he said, "Yeah I will, one day, when this happens, if that happens". The result is that he's still stuck in no man's land doing what he's doing.

The grass may always seem greener on the other side of the fence, but when you get to the other side, you realize that you face similar challenges and issues. It's for you to decide what you want to do with your life. You control what you want. Nobody else decides that for you. Emotionally, nobody has the right to make you feel bad about yourself except yourself. You set your own benchmark and expectations. YES, ONLY YOU.

Are your goals a must or are they a should?

How many times has each of us been guilty of promising people we love, or worse still, ourselves, that it is time to lose weight, to paint the house, to quit smoking, to take the garbage out, to learn a foreign language by year end, to go for a vacation, but only to fail to follow through when the time comes? How often has each of us set New Year's resolutions on the first day of the year only to end up reflecting back on the unachieved goals and resolutions 365 days later? I know I have. The reason why this happens is because when you set these goals, you set them as a SHOULD, not as a MUST. You tell yourself you should quit smoking, after you light up the next cigarette? Or you tell yourself you should lose weight, after you finish the chocolate bar? These goals only serve as a "should" and will not work, since "should" does not give you a sense of purpose and reason to achieve these goals. The important key here is to stop lying to yourself. When you tell yourself you're going to do something and then you don't, you let yourself down.

Rephrase your goals! Start thinking in MUST MODE. Tell yourself you must quit smoking or else… You must lose weight or else… Give yourself enough purpose and reason to follow through with your goals. Challenge yourself. Use what YOU KNOW will work for you. Write a list of 10 reasons why you must absolutely quit smoking. Keep this list close by where it's visible and you will absolutely see it and get it ingrained in your mind. For example, if your goal is to quit smoking as it is burning a hole in your financial pocket, set your goal as "Each time I light up a cigarette I commit myself to giving $5 to my friend, or my wife". Get them to sign an agreement if you need to. I'm sure they would be more than happy to help you out. For this to work, you must be totally honest with yourself. YOU DECIDE. Make it as interesting as possible. You know what works best for you. You know what makes you tick.

If you have decided that you must lose weight because it is affecting your health, you may want to set your goal like this: "Each time I go for that additional brownie or chocolate bar, I will allow my friend or loved ones to reprimand me in a way that they see fit". Of course these reprimands must be objective and reasonable. Think of these chocolate bars and brownies as a form of crime. If you pride yourself on personal achievement and respect, announce to your friends that you are on a program to lose weight. Each time you fail to adhere to these restrictions, you put yourself on the line. Think of the promise you have made to them and the respect you will lose if you fail to follow through with your promise. In other words, you will have no choice but to walk the talk. Again, this method will only work if you are totally honest with yourself. YOU DECIDE. I am using these two examples as they are the two top goals that people set but fail to follow through.

In short, if you don't give yourself an option to fail, you will follow through. You will meet that mark. You will achieve what you want. You put yourself in MUST MODE. Are you excited yet? I know I am! Next we are going to see how we are able to achieve this with a proper plan and procedure!

Four Steps To Achieving Your Goals

Now that you have decided that the goals you set are a MUST and placed yourself in MUST MODE, let us move on to the next section on how to systematically set these goals using four simple steps:

1. Come up with a blueprint plan of what you want to achieve;
2. Take action on the plan that you have set your mind upon;
3. Review your plans periodically and receive feedback;

4. Take action and keep evaluating your plan until you achieve the desired results.

Come Up With A Blueprint Plan Of What You Want To Achieve

Now let's do a bit of exercise. Get a pen and a notepad ready. Choose a place where it's quiet and you are able to concentrate, without distractions or disruptions. Lock yourself in a room if you have to. Your mobile phone should be turned off, so your friends won't be able to reach you during this time. You should be doing this exercise during your most productive hours. Now, list down as many goals and targets that you would like to achieve. Remember, these goals must be specific like "I must lose five kilos" or "I must earn $20,000 a month" or "I must ask my lovely colleague Debbie out for a movie". Avoid goals or targets that are general, such as "I would like to earn more", "I would like to lose weight" and so on and so forth. You get the picture. Also, these goals can be for any aspect of life, be it financial, emotional, spiritual, social or economical. Don't worry about how you will be able to achieve them at this point in time. Just focus on the goals that you have been thinking about all this while but have never put on paper. Jot down any thoughts and ideas that just appear in your mind. You mustn't let anything distract you. Take as much time as you need. You can also use the spreadsheet provided on page 75.

Next, pick out five goals from the list that you most desire and want to achieve. These five goals must be the ones you have craved to achieve in the past but haven't made the necessary effort to follow through. On the next page of your notepad, make three columns and title each column short-term, medium-term and long-term. Now a short-term goal is a goal or a target that can be achieved in one day to three months. A medium-term goal is a goal or a target that can be achieved in three months to one year. A long-term goal is a goal or a target achievable in one year or longer, depending on the magnanimity of the goal.

Take Action On The Plan That You Have Set Your Mind Upon

Once you have listed all the short, medium, and long-term goals, I want you to write down next to each goal, how each can be achieved in a clear step-by-step maneuver. These steps must include the breakdown of the time it would take to do each thing. See illustrations below for a sample of the spreadsheet that you can use. You may modify this spreadsheet according to your personal requirements to complete the tasks in a more convenient way. In this section, you will need to include how you know when you have achieved each outcome or goal: what is defined as the goal being achieved, how you will feel, what you will get. Be as specific as possible. Most people who have no specific goals, are not sure when they have achieved a certain goal as they have no specific target and no time frame. Repeat this process for your medium as well as your long-term goals. The key here is to keep the step-by-step process on how you will achieve part of each goal, as specific as possible. Like a jigsaw puzzle, you will need to find the matching pieces to get the entire picture. It's the same with goals. We need to break them down to smaller and more manageable pieces.

A lot of people have been asking questions like: how can I be successful, how can I achieve my dreams, how can I do this and how can I do that? Simply put, in order to be successful, emulate every single step and action that your mentors take. Clearly, they are your mentors for some reason. They are successful in their own right, and perhaps you admire them and want to be just like them. Why not?

When Tony Fernandes wanted to start a budget airline seven years ago, he couldn't get a license or anybody to buy his idea. You see, the idea of a discount carrier couldn't sell since everybody had the mindset that flying is only for people who can afford it. He then sold his idea to the Prime Minister at the time. He envisioned how a discount carrier would revolutionize Asian air travel, at a time when airlines worldwide were still struggling from the impact of September 11 terrorist attacks.

He took a substantial risk by buying the airline for a token of 26 cents, as well as inheriting its debt of roughly $11 million. He only saw one outcome. He could not afford to fail. Fernandes learned to think like an entrepreneur from his mentor, Sir Richard Branson. He imitated and emulated what Branson was doing and followed his successful business model. Fernandes had a remarkable influence on the shaping of government and airline mentality in Southeast Asia and beyond. Previously, neighboring countries had never had any kind of open-skies agreement. He knew exactly what he wanted and had a clear idea and vision of how to achieve it.

In order to do just that, focus on what the person you want to emulate is doing right. Emulate his method from the planning process to the development phase. If you need to, modify the steps to suit your own personal goals. What may take a few years to accomplish could even be shortened to a few months if done properly. Do note that sometimes, you can even do things better than your mentor. This is because most of what your mentor has done was based on trial and error. You can do better because you have already seen the impact and experienced the results of what has become of his plan. Therefore, you can plan better and definitely attain better results.

Once you have set your sight on the step-by-step process of how to achieve each goal with specific details, ACT ON IT. Get into the action habit. Start with a smaller goal or task and follow the step-by-step process that you have written down. After all, these are your own handwritten instructions and who else will better understand them than yourself? Stick the piece of paper or spreadsheet somewhere visible to you when you wake up, before you go to work, while at your daily routines and before you go to bed at night. Get it ingrained into your memory and read it out loud at least five times a day. Make a commitment to yourself (and others if required) to set a specific amount of time each day to achieve the goal you have come up with. You will notice that an amazing thing will happen. You will find yourself become more aware of your current surroundings, more aware of how much time you have to yourself. Why? Because you keep track of your goals that you have set. Don't just take my word for it! Try it! Repeat this for each of the goals that you have listed in the short, medium and long-term columns.

Procrastination

Procrastination is the common enemy, which every man must conquer. It is the habit of putting off and delaying certain tasks and responsibilities that you know you should have done. This happens because your goals are not clear or specific enough so that even when you list them, you don't know how to start achieving them, thus delaying action until the last minute. This leads to mediocre results. Procrastination can also happen when you underestimate the complexity of the issue at hand, hence no adequate research is done before setting a reasonable and realistic plan and time frame to achieve the goal.

Every one is guilty of procrastinating at one time or another. No one, and I mean no one, can operate at 100% productivity all the time. All of us need a break to avoid burn out. The key is to recognize when you are procrastinating, and what you can do to avoid it. Ask yourself these questions: do you keep putting off tasks and/or responsibilities which you know you must complete by a certain time, or do you wait until the very last minute when you have no other options? Are you very indecisive, change directions and make different decisions at the first sign of trouble? Do you need to wait for a special occasion or time of the day, for example after lunch, after dinner or worse still, an anniversary, a best friend's birthday and so on, before starting a task? If the answers to these questions are mostly yes, then you are indeed a procrastinator.

To beat procrastination, you need to be able to prioritize things that need to get done each day. Having a list of goals in a step-by-step process is a start. I have developed a spreadsheet with the time line for you. After completing each of the items on the list, you must reward yourself with a break or time out session. Ensure that these breaks are included in the time line to avoid unnecessary delays in achieving your goals.

Beating procrastination is all about properly managing your time and effectively using time to get more things done. Keep a time log so that you are aware of how much time you have spent on each activity every day during the course of the goal achievement. To keep a time log, include information such as the tasks that you do daily or weekly depending on your particular goal: short, medium or long-term. See the example below for information you may require:

- Name of the task that you want to get done.
- How long you estimate it will take and the actual time taken. This is to gauge accuracy of the time that you have allocated to each task.
- Interruptions, if applicable. If yes, include what the interruptions were and how long.
- Is there anyone else involved? Are you capable of completing the task? Is completion of tasks dependent on a third party?

Next, you need to be able to categorize your activities into meaningful areas such as family, career, hobbies, passion, friends, and so on and so forth. You can distribute these categories by deciding how many hours you plan to put in for each. Note that this doesn't mean you have to allocate a certain amount of time each day for each category. Some categories may only come in during the weekends, like hobbies or passion.

After having done this for a few days, you will find that a lot of the time you spend each day is wasted on unproductive activities. You can then decide whether to eliminate those activities and free up more of your time to complete your goals and tasks on time. However, at the end of each day, ensure that the amount of time allocated to each category you have specified, is realistic and in accordance to what you believe and value.

Review Your Plans Periodically And Receive Feedback

Once you have initiated your first goal and put it into action mode, you need to keep track of progress: how well you are doing and whether you are on course of achieving the goal you have set based on the step-by-step processes that you have determined earlier. For instance if your goal is to get the whole house painted and cleaned in one week, you may want to review your goal and plans on a daily basis to ensure that you remain on top of things and don't slack off. Getting the whole house painted may involve painting the garage, painting all the rooms, painting the living room and getting it decorated and so on.

Therefore, in order to know that you are on track, follow the step-by-step plan you have listed in your 7-day goal and periodically review it. If you realize you are getting side tracked by certain unexpected turns of events, which will happen however full proof you think your plans are, allow yourself some time off so that you are able to review, realign and readjust the goals and targets that you have initially set. Be realistic enough and allow yourself some amendments to the goal that you have set to be on par with current situations. The key here is to use the written down goals as a stepping stone, as a way to gauge your productivity level, to enable you to visualize what you want to achieve.

If the goal set is one of longer duration, say a medium-term goal in the initial blueprint plan, it may take 1 to 3 months. You may want to make the periodic review every week or fortnight to ensure that you remain on track. Do what is required to amend and readjust the plans within those 3 months so that you can achieve the goal. Repeat this process as well for all the other goals whether they are long-term goals or short and you'll be able to see results in no time! Bear in mind that good leaders are able to take challenges as they come along rather than worry about them in the blueprint plan.

Take Action And Keep Evaluating Your Plan Until You Achieve The Desired Results

When you review your goals you may need to do certain adjustments in order to achieve them. Justify to yourself why you are making the amendments. Be aware of the reasons for each amendment. Don't amend these goals because you have procrastinated and failed to follow through with your own plan. This is why I have shared with you a small section on procrastination and how to beat it by keeping a time log of your daily, weekly or monthly activities, whichever is applicable.

As soon as amendments and/or adjustments have been made, continue to take action until you have reached your objectives. Again, you need to define what is the outcome or definition that you know you will see once the goal is achieved; or else you may not even realize that you have reached the goal. More often than not, you will feel frustrated and tend to give up easily. This is the result of goals not being specific enough. When necessary, repeat steps three and four until you are satisfied with the end result of the particular goal you have set.

Repeat this for all goals. If you do this with great consistency, your life will change dramatically to the way you desire it.

See the destination before you start the journey

During the time of President Abraham Lincoln who fought so hard for equality among all citizens in the United States, no one would have envisioned that over a hundred years later, an African-American would be in the running to be the president of the United States.

This is what evolution in the human mentality has brought us. Barack Obama, an African-American from a modest home, stands as the first African-American president of the United States.

Obama grew up in much less privileged circumstances – abandoned by his Kenyan father at the age of two, his mother divorced twice, while he grew up with the help of his grandparents who had moved to Hawaii. His humble origins are a classic example of the American dream of achieving success from poor beginnings.

You may have started slower than the rest. You may be less privileged compared to others. But if you are committed to getting what you want, impossible is no longer a word you will understand or accept. You will simply keep going until you achieve what you set out to do. Trust me. It will work in the end.

It's not where you start in life, it's where you end up. It doesn't matter where you are right now. It matters where you want to be. See the destination before you start the journey. You can be waiting on tables now and doing 15-hours shifts on a daily basis. I'm not saying there is no honor in that. Doing any honest work that pays modestly is miles better than doing something against the law.

As long as you have a plan, what you are doing now is only temporary. When all your plans fall into place, you will see that the sacrifices you have made so far will start to bear fruit. Good things come to those who are patient. Luck is when preparation meets opportunity. When you are well prepared, the opportunity automatically presents itself. You'll be able to identify it even from the scantiest of hints.

As Stephen R. Covey famously put in his book *Seven Habits of Highly Effective People*, "To begin with the end in mind is a very simple concept that many of us fail to put into use or do so at the wrong time". Have you ever received a call from a friend who asked you for directions to a restaurant, your house or a place that you're familiar with? Sure you have! When you give the directions to your friend, you visualize the roads you use to get there, the U-turn you make when you reach a traffic light, the left or the right turn at a specific landmark. You are able to see the destination even when you don't make the trip. Or have you ever planned a vacation with your loved ones or friends to an exotic location or a resort? In the midst of planning, you get all the information for the vacation and start to imagine the great fun it will be when you actually reach there. On the day of the vacation, you get even more excited and get an adrenalin rush from thinking about what you are going to do once you have reached the resort. You are able to see the destination before you have even started the holiday. Now why is this so? As I mentioned previously, when you start gathering information on the resort, your subconscious mind kicks off into imagination mode and you start to imagine all the things you will do based on this information, the experience from previous trips if any, and also sentiments, comments and opinions from people who have been there. I personally remember the first time I started planning for my vacation to Bali, Indonesia. The moment I decided to go to Bali, I began to research as much as I could about possible places of interest to visit, the culture, the food and the people that I would meet. I asked friends who have made the trip about what to eat, where to go and what to look out for. On the day of the trip, I started visualizing how wonderful Bali is, and what fun it will be to stroll along the white sand beaches of Kuta with my group of friends. When I arrived, everything materialized into exactly what I had imagined. Bear in mind that I have never been to Bali before! Here I used the power of visualization to see the destination before I started the journey. Similarly, if I had received negative comments on Bali, my imagination would have centered on them, and I probably would not have taken the trip.

Seeing the destination before you start the journey is based on a concept that all things are created twice: the mental creation and the physical creation. Genting Highlands founder, the late Lim Goh Tong started his vision of the Highlands resort cum casino as a dream, a desire and a visualization that was cultivated into reality with consistent effort, hard work and perseverance. When a businessman founds a company, whether selling a product or service, it all starts with an idea or a concept that was visualized and acted upon to realize it. A hundred years ago, who would have heard of taxi drivers, babysitters, call centre operators and hundreds of other occupations that have boomed in modern times? All these started from ideas and were acted upon consistently until the desired results were produced. When you want to build a house, you have a vision of how you want your dream home to be, you then hire an architect to design, make the blueprint plans, and then find a developer to turn the house into reality. If you are a manager and want to have a meeting with your staff, you set an agenda and expect them to come up with solutions, ideas and concepts. You prepare for the meeting and know what to expect from your staff.

To varying degrees, most people use this principle in more ways and areas in their life than they realize. Depending on the level of understanding of the two levels, namely mental creation and physical creation, we will determine how we can act upon the mental creation to materialize it in the physical creation.

> *"You see things and ask why? I dream of things that never were and say, why not?"*
>
> – George Bernard Shaw –

SMART Goals

When we set goals and targets, we need to make sure that all the goals and targets are Specific, Measurable, Achievable, Realistic and Tangible; in other words, SMART goals.

Specific Goals

Specific goals are goals which are clear, concise and have a greater chance of getting accomplished compared to general goals. A general goal would be: "I would like to earn more money". A specific goal would be: "I want to increase my level of income to $8,000 a month". To set specific goals, you have to answer what I call the 5-wives and 1-husband questions:

- Who?

  Who must achieve this goal? Who is involved in the process of achieving this goal? Is this an individual goal or a team goal? How many people need to work together to achieve it?

- What?

  What do you want to accomplish? Ask yourself the purpose of setting up this goal in the first place. What exactly do you want to accomplish? Remember to be as specific as possible. What are the possible constraints or challenges on the way to achieving this goal?

- When?

  For each goal to be realized, you must have a time frame of when you want to achieve it. As mentioned earlier, you divide the goals into short, medium and long-term. If you don't have an idea on when the goals should be achieved, the goal will be nothing more than a dream, buried deep inside your mind with no chance of being realized.

- Which?

Which requirements do you have to fulfill to match that goal? Which steps do you need to take to achieve what you want?

- Why?

List down specific reasons on why you must achieve your goal. State the benefits you will receive and advantages you will have upon achieving each goal.

- How?

This is similar to the four-step process on how you can achieve your goal. You must have a plan, and this plan must be specific with a time frame to follow.

Measurable Goals

You need to be able to measure the progress of your goal in order to achieve it. When you measure your progress, you keep track of dates, you stay on track and are able to achieve satisfaction each time a hurdle is overcome as you approach the attainment of your goal. In this way you will have a clear visual and will feel the exhilaration that spurs you on further to the achievement of your goal.

To ensure that your goals are measurable, you have to ask questions such as: How much? How far? How will I know when I have achieved my goal? How will I feel?

Attainable Goals

When you have identified the short, medium and long-term goals, you begin to plan the four-step process on how you can make that goal become a reality. You start developing the technical acumen and necessary beliefs. You look for opportunities to bring yourself closer to the realization of your goals.

You can attain ANY goal, regardless of the size if you follow the four-step process and establish a realistic time frame. Keep in mind that it's not resources, but resourcefulness that determines your achievement. With these steps, goals that seem impossible look more reasonable and manageable, not because your goals change, but because you grow and evolve to match the size of those goals.

Realistic Goals

Realistic goals are goals in which you must believe in. You must believe you can realize them with proper planning and willingness to work on that plan. There is no goal which is impossible, but the manner in which it is carried out makes the difference. For instance, if you tell everybody that you are going to lose 20 pounds in a day, you will end up disappointed and ridiculed. You need not worry if nobody else has achieved the goal you are setting. With proper and meticulous planning, you are able to achieve anything that you put your mind to. After all, this is how athletes break world records and set the benchmark for their peers to follow.

Tangible Goals

A tangible goal can be experienced with one of the sensory mechanisms like taste, touch, smell, hearing and sight. For instance, if you set yourself a target of making $20,000 a month, once you get that pay check or when your bank balance swells up to that amount, you know you have achieved your goal. When the goal is tangible, you have a much better chance of achieving it.

With SMART goals, you don't have to worry about setting goals which are unrealistic. You have greater control over what you want, when you want and how you want it.

Stretch Goals To Stretch Your Imagination

One of the most powerful techniques that marketing and advertisement people use for motivation and to excite people about their products and services, are two words: *possibility* and *hope*. Imagine the possibility of earning $20,000. Imagine the possibility of realizing the craziest dream that you've ever had. Hope is what drives people forward – hope of finding the perfect partner, hope of winning the lottery and hope of living your dream.

Similarly, stretch goals are goals that at the time you set them, may seem impossible to reach by means of current abilities and skills. But the thought of reaching them gives you an adrenalin rush and a sense of emotional drive. Most of us tend to set incremental or puny goals. Incremental goals are goals that are slightly higher or bigger that what you currently have. For example, we will use your salary range as a good indication. You set yourself the target of achieving an additional 10% on your salary. Is that enough to excite you? Will that give you the emotional drive to jump into action? Hardly.

Setting crazy stretch goals unfold your imagination to dream the impossible. And when that happens, your mind starts to think of ways to make that possibility a reality. You start to explore what is possible, and think out of the box.

Note that in SMART goals, you have one section called realistic goals. Now don't get me wrong. Crazy stretch goals are absolutely realistic. How are we able to achieve all our goals? When you set stretch goals, you set stretch plans. That means you think out of the box to ensure that your goals are achieved! Ask yourself, what can I do that is different from others? What am I passionate about? What do I love to do that I can spend hours doing repeatedly? If I could do anything in the world, what would it be? Instead of asking yourself how you can develop in the team, ask yourself how you can develop in the company. Instead of asking yourself how you can develop in the company, ask yourself how you can develop in the industry. Instead of asking yourself how you can develop in the industry, ask yourself how you can develop in the country. Instead of asking yourself how you can develop in the country, ask yourself how you can develop in the region, continent, and of course the world. When you think like that, you get to see things from a different perspective, from a rounded and general view of what is possible.

Short Term Goal (less than 3 months)

Start Date: _____

Stop Date: _____

Goal 1: _____

_____

_____

_____

Steps on how to achieve it: _____

_____

_____

_____

Achieved: YES ☐
           NO ☐

If NO, please justify why and fill up revised date.

Reason: _____

_____

Revised Date: _____

Name: _____

Signature: _____

Date: _____

*Note that revised date must be <4 weeks from Stop Date to avoid procrastination.

Medium Term Goal (more than 3 months, less than 6 months)

Start Date: _____

Stop Date: _____

Goal 1: _____

_____

_____

_____

Steps on how to achieve it: _____

_____

_____

_____

Review Date 1: _____

On track: YES ☐
            NO ☐

If NO, please justify why and fill up revised date.

Reason: _____

_____

Revised Date: _____

Review Date 2: _____

On track: YES ☐
            NO ☐

If NO, please justify why and fill up revised date.

Reason: _____

_____

Revised Date: _____

Review Date 3: _____

On track: YES ☐
           NO ☐

If NO, please justify why and fill up revised date.

Reason: _____

_____

Revised Date: _____

Achieved: YES ☐
           NO ☐

If NO, please justify why and fill up revised date.

Reason: _____

_____

Revised Date: _____

Name: _____

Signature: _____

Date: ___ _____

*Note that review date must be between 4-8 weeks from Start Date to ensure the goal is up to date and current. Subsequently, the next review date should also be the same duration so that you are up to date on your goal and is able to keep the momentum going.

IV
DESIRE: FUEL FOR YOUR SUCCESS

"A clear vision, backed by definite plans and desire, accomplish far more in a shorter period of time than people without them could ever imagine"

– Brian Tracy –

We often hear of people who desire to be better in every way: from making more money (the most common), to being productive in their work, losing weight, being more committed to their family, spending more time with their children, to doing more charity for society. The list is endless. But how deep actually is their desire to achieve these dreams? Is it just another new year's resolution that will be forgotten two weeks later? Is it just another empty promise given to the spouse hoping he or she will stop mumbling? The truth is these desires and goals are nothing but desire. There is no concrete action plan to fulfill these dreams and make them into reality.

Have you ever been put down by people saying that you are simply good for nothing? Or been criticized by friends and peers who do not feel you are capable of doing the things that you have planned?

At a time when actors and actresses projected an image of good looks and great bodies, it sure did not stop this one guy from getting where he knew he wanted to be. Born with slurred speech due to birth complications, causing partial paralysis and a drooping lower lip, this individual knew that he wanted to be an actor when he was young. He even dropped out of school as he was about to graduate just to start his acting career! Talk about extreme measures! Sylvester Stallone got his inspiration for his first movie, *Rocky*, an underdog boxer who goes through adversity and hardship to triumph over his more illustrious opponent, by watching a boxing match between Muhammad Ali and Chuck Wepner. He then went home and wrote the script in 72 hours!

He went to one production company after another, and none accepted his script. They even told him that his script would be a box office flop. Finally, one company agreed to buy his script and wanted to sign a more popular actor as the lead actor. But Stallone knew that he was an actor and not a writer and managed to persuade the company to give him the lead role. It was rumored that when he was struggling to launch his acting career, he sold his pet dog just to make ends meet! After the success of *Rocky*, he bought back the dog from the new owner for multiple times the price he sold it for. So successful and inspirational was *Rocky* that the Governor of Philadelphia even had a statue of Rocky erected at the Rocky steps where Stallone trained in the movie!

Stallone then went on to write, direct and star in several other movies which have made him an international icon. Not bad for someone who had paralysis and could not talk properly, and was shunned by people, one after another! So deep was his commitment and faith that he knew if he kept going, he was going to make it, no matter what.

It is the same no matter what goal you set: if you have enough faith and desire for what you want to do, success will just take care of itself. Never let anyone tell you what you can not do. Allowing yourself to fulfill your dreams only occurs in the absence of doubt.

Desire is the motivating force that governs our daily actions, as much as we hate to admit it in many cases. Someone once said that each human act, be it good or bad, is prompted by desire. A person can be kind because he desires to be kind. Likewise, another person can be cruel because he desires to be such. You desire to be slim and fit, and yet you grab yourself a chocolate brownie on your way to work? Why is that so? Because your desire for that chocolate brownie is far greater than the desire to get back in shape. Everything we do is prompted by desire, high and low. Desire is the motivating factor behind all actions. In the preceding chapters I said motivation is what gets us started, habit is what keeps us going. The tiny difference between two individuals is how deep their desire is and how far they are willing to go to achieve it.

An experience or an event is only as powerful as the meaning that we give to it. A society misfit, addictive gambler and occasional drug pusher who has attempted suicide a few times, is serving a jail sentence today for credit card forgery. He has two sons, born four years apart, one who grew up to be just like him, convicted of theft and drug pushing and is now also in jail. His elder son, however, has led a totally different life. Married to a beautiful and dedicated woman, he has three children and a challenging career that requires him to travel to other continents. He goes to the gym regularly, has no alcohol or drug addiction and does not smoke! Now the million dollar question is: how come these two men, having grown up in virtually the same environment, turned out so differently? When questioned, both of them provided the same answer, "How else could I have turned out, having come from a broken family with an abusive father?" These two men gave different meanings to the same events that have surrounded their lives. The younger one decided to follow in his father's footsteps, thinking that his father was to be blamed for his upbringing, and there was no way he could change for the better. On the other hand, the elder brother decided to empower himself, even though surrounded with the bitter experience of his childhood, and as a constant reminder of how NOT to be like his father when he grew up.

So often we are led to believe that events and experience shape us into who we are today. It is not the events or the experience but the meaning and beliefs we give those events. Our desire to change the meaning will determine whether we are successful or otherwise.

Everything we do is preceded by our desire to act in order to make it happen. In order to desire something, you must believe that you will benefit or get a certain expected result from it. For instance, you desire to study because you want to pass an exam. You desire to go to work because you need the money to pay the bills. You desire to eat because you feel hungry. Everything, from the time you wake up till the time you close your eyes is precipitated with desire, be it high or low.

From time to time, many people including myself are stuck in a particular situation in life because of the desire to avoid pain. We know what needs to be done to achieve our goal, but simply put the goal to the back because we know we have to sacrifice something before achieving it. Some feel that making a change, even a positive one, would cause too much discomfort and take too much time. Hence, complacency creeps in and people settle down in the state they are currently in. When quizzed, these are the people who give the most excuses and blame others rather than themselves. Common excuses are: "I will never have that much time", "that person is just fortunate that he is from a wealthy family", etc. Most people today prefer instant gratification from what they get. This is how credit card companies make more money every year. They encourage cardholders to spend first and pay later.

The concept of desire is simple. When your desire is weak, it is unlikely that anything will motivate you to act towards accomplishing something. If your desire is strong, nothing will stop you from successfully attaining what you want. To have a strong desire, visualize positive thoughts of what will happen when you achieve your goal. Repeat the visualization at least 10 times and you will begin to see a difference in your physiology. You will feel better and have more confidence. Likewise, if you keep manifesting negative thoughts on how you are unable to achieve something, you will feel dreadful and lose the desire to achieve what you have set out to do. For the purpose of illustration, start visualizing your top three goals that you want to achieve. Repeat this at least 10 times, with a clear step-by-step on how to achieve them. You will begin to notice that your physiology and emotional state start changing for the better.

This desire especially applies to sporting icons, athletes that compete in sports such as tennis and racing. You can question any of them, and I bet that each one will give you the same answer. When they enter a tournament, they expect to win it and visualize themselves holding aloft the trophy many times before the competition actually starts. This is why you get athletes and teams who, on paper, are inferior compared to their opponents but end up beating them. So what is the reason? In a word, desire. Their desire to outclass, outrun, outflank the opponents far outweighs the other teams' desire and of course, their physiology changes and performance speaks for itself.

Letting Go Of The Past Is Only Possible With Great Desires

Letting go of the past means changing your life for the better, not leaning back on memories of yesteryears, comparing your past achievements or failures with where you currently are. Are you one of those people who get haunted by memories of the past? Whose mind keeps lingering on a certain experience, especially a bad one, a broken relationship, a failed business, the loss of a loved one and much more? Do you often ask yourself if only or what if I would have done things differently before? Could things have happened differently? Do you resort to going through some particular experience over and over again and spending hours mulling over what could have been?

If your answers are "yes", fear not, for you are not alone. There are millions of people out there who are just like you, thinking of their past glories or failures without realizing that they are wasting their present time away. These people continually ask themselves what ifs and try to comprehend what went wrong. They feel a great sense of remorse and regret over a failed relationship or how they could have been a better partner, a more loving father, a more successful businessperson and so on. Remember that regret only happens when you are not able to move forward from past mistakes, and you get stuck in the past by blaming yourself. When people lock their minds into this state of denial and keep repeating the bitter memories that clog their thoughts, they fall into depression.

You should not have to feel this way. Because when you focus on the past, you deny yourself the present and the future. To let go of the past, you first need to have the desire to focus on what you want in life. In Chapter III, I have shown you how powerful goals are and how to achieve them. Start thinking forward. Give yourself the only option that is of moving forward.

In order to have the desire to move forward, first you need to take responsibility for what happened in the past. Please take note that taking responsibility for what happened does not mean taking the blame for what happened in your relationship, family or in whatever business failure that you've had. It's about acknowledging the fact that you were part of the whole event and perhaps played a role in whatever happened.

If you keep thinking about a past relationship and wondering how it could have been better, you are never going to get out of it emotionally and mentally. First of all, you need to acknowledge that the relationship did come to an end and while it may be true, you may be the one who has caused the failure of the relationship. If you weren't in the relationship in the first place, there wouldn't have been any breakup. Analyze with a clear mind what went wrong, how you are going to change and let this relationship go. When analyzing what went wrong, do not focus on the wrongs that you did but rather on how you can do things better the next time. Move forward, and make a commitment to yourself: when you get into another relationship in the future, you will not make the same mistake again. Learn from the past, it is a great teacher.

The reason why I am focusing on failed relationships is because they are the most common reason people derail from their current goals and accomplishments.

Another common situation is losing a job and having a family of five to feed as you are the sole breadwinner. It's time to stop wallowing in self-pity. Take responsibility for what happened. Do not accept the blame by saying you were not good enough for the job, or asking yourself why you did not see it coming. Instead, take responsibility by committing yourself to finding another job, a better one, and make sure that if there is any retrenchment, you are going to be the one that gets promoted and not pushed out the door.

Everybody has their own demons. It's in how we exorcise them that determines how we can be a better person when the same experiences recur. Every past event, be it pleasant or otherwise, teaches us some value to be carried forward into the future.

Once you shift your focus from the past to the present, your mind will automatically let go of the past. There will be times when you feel down, or alone, or things don't seem to go right, and your mind starts wandering back to the past. When this happens, immediately snap your fingers and tell yourself, "hey that's in the past, I am here now, and totally focused on my goals and the present moment and my new life". Slowly but surely, you will notice that the past no longer haunts you like it used to. Of course you will not stop thinking of the past right away. But as you reaffirm what you want to do, what your goals are, your mind will definitely adjust itself to its new surroundings. That's why it is so important and vital to write down your desires and goals and stick them where you will not miss them. Every day, read to yourself out loud the goals you've written down and you will notice that your mind will slowly focus on what you want it to focus on: the present moment.

Another important note that I want to highlight is that you can change the way you see past events. Find a positive thought to describe how some past experience has made you who you are today. No matter how bitter that experience was, focus and force yourself to come up with at least one positive sentence to say about that experience. Be it someone you hate, a trip to your in-laws or the death of a loved one. I am not asking you to lie to yourself, but merely to see that experience from another perspective, from another pair of shoes so to speak. There are always two ways of looking at the same topic, no matter how specific that topic is. For example: $1 + 1 = 2$ and $5 - 3 = 2$. Besides, how do you know the way you see things right now is the correct way? Remember, it's just the way you interpret it. Nothing more, nothing less. You are what you think you are. With your thoughts you shape your world.

Your current perception may be to view things negatively. But again, how do you know what you think is real? It's just the way you see something based on past references that you have had or read about or heard about somewhere, someplace, to make you think your interpretation is correct. Change the way you see things. Change your perception and the reality unfolds. Search for new references and evidence of a similar experience but in a positive way. For more information, you may look at Chapter I.

Understand that you are where you are now because of past events, because of decisions that you have made. Now focus on this moment, focus on exactly what it is that you want and you will eventually take the next step to be exactly where you need to be in the future. Learn from the past, focus on the present and prepare for the future.

One final step in letting go of your past is to start thinking in the NOW mode. Take a look at what you want to achieve in life. Think about the goals and start paying attention to the thoughts that you have about achieving those goals. Are these thoughts hindering you from achieving those goals? Are they in conflict with your goals? If they are, you will never achieve those goals until you learn to realign them with your thought patterns.

Sit down in a quiet place and write down all the negative thought patterns that you have, as well as negative beliefs that have been holding you back. The list may surprise you! What you uncover may actually determine your chances for

> *By repeating your thought patterns and reaffirming them over and over again, they become embedded in your subconscious mind and eventually become your reality. That is why you need to be careful what you think and believe because that is what you will get."*
>
> *— Anthony Robbins —*

success. Now, see if those beliefs and negative thoughts are hindering you from achieving what you want. After that, start developing positive thought patterns and positive beliefs to replace the negative ones. Repeat this process in your mind and reaffirm it over and over again. Learn it by heart if you need to. Keep it in your wallet where it is easily reachable and can be referred to whenever the negative thoughts start creeping back.

Desire equals dreams?

It's important that along the way to achieving your dreams you realize that you will be enabling not only your dreams, but also the dreams of others. Randy Pausch, a professor of computer science at the Carnegie Melon University, put it best, when he said that you will feel much better, even if you fail to achieve your dreams, if you help others achieve theirs. What were your childhood dreams? Did you dream of meeting Bugs Bunny? Or your superhero? I know I dreamt of being just like Superman with super powers, saving people's lives. Among some of Pausch's dreams was to experience zero gravity and to meet one of his childhood idols, Star Trek Captain! And he managed to achieve those dreams because he believed in them badly enough that he did anything he could conceive to make those dreams a reality.

In his lecture, *Really Achieving Your Childhood Dreams*, he asked the crowd to think deeply about what matters to them and added, "What wisdom would you try to impart to the rest of the world if you knew it was your last chance?"

It's important that each of us has specific dreams which we desire to achieve. To start, we have to know where we want to go, what we want to do and how to go about starting out.

Along life's little journey, you will hit brick wall after brick wall. Brick walls or challenges are there for a reason. They are there to stop "THE OTHER PEOPLE" who do not want badly enough to achieve their dreams and desires. Challenges are there to show our dedication to a cause that we believe in, and how strong our beliefs are.

Another lesson to remember is that when you do something wrong, you will have critics coming out and lashing out at you as if you murdered somebody. You may feel down and guilty at the same time, and may not even be so forthcoming in your next task. When you screw up and nobody cares enough to tell you about it, it means they have given up on you already. It also means that they no longer care about you anymore. Your critics are the ones who love you and show that they care. It's true. How else would I be able to see how far I have come, if there wasn't anyone out there who bothered to tell me where I am going, if what I am doing is correct, or what I can improve on to make things better. Now you know that when your parents give you long lectures about coming home late, mixing with the wrong crowd and so forth, is just because they love you enough to spend the time telling you about it.

So when you receive criticism from a fellow friend or colleague, stop and think for one moment how you can convert that criticism into constructive feedback that you can use to improve your life and the lives of others.

It's amazing how enthusiasm can help transform people's lives for the better. Experience is what you get when you did not get what you wanted. If you messed up along the way, fell down, knocked against a brick wall, you might either give up or settle for little. DON'T. When you do not always get what you want, reflect on what you have gone through and how you can be better next time a similar challenge appears or the same brick wall shows up and tries to knock you out of your stride. Remember, regret only comes when you do not learn anything from your past experience and make the same mistake twice. People who have learned to pick themselves up from past experiences do not make the same mistake twice.

Have you ever heard of the term "head fake"? It's a term that is commonly used in basketball when a player tries to deceive the opponent's defender by pretending to move in one direction and then switches to the other direction instead. It's an interesting concept in life where we end up learning something else along the way or journey to our goals. Sometimes, what we pick up along the way becomes even more precious than the destination point.

You can call it head fake learning. When you enroll yourself in swimming lessons, or attend football coaching clinics, you indirectly pick up other skills besides the main goal of learning how to swim, or learning how to dribble better. You learn to interact with other people, you learn the meaning of perseverance, you learn the importance of

> *"Do not be afraid of the space between your dreams and reality. If you can dream it, you can make it so"*
>
> *– Belva Davis –*

teamwork, which is priceless, and you learn how to work together in a competitive environment. Most of all, you enjoy yourself. And ultimately, you learn how to swim and dribble better. A lot of our life's lessons are picked up using this technique where most of our learning capabilities are honed through our subconscious mind without us even realizing it. It forms the core of our beliefs and when a similar experience occurs again, we will know how to go about handling the situation in a calmer manner.

In this chapter, I am focusing a lot on the word *desire* as it has a strong correlation between our beliefs and how we can achieve what we want by manifesting and channeling our desire the right way. First, we are going to identify what the desires are, how much attention we are giving our desires and if we are allowing our desires to happen with our daily actions.

Have you watched the movie, *The Pursuit of Happiness* starring Will Smith as Chris Gardner? It's based on a true and indeed very heart-warming story about a salesman who turned a corner, changed his life forever and went from rags to riches. Before he made his first million, Gardner was selling medical equipment with great difficulty. Then he found his passion in trading and stock broking and got glued to it. The rest, as they say, is history.

While Gardner was attending his internship program at Dean Witter Reynolds in 1981, he spent a year in the streets with his two-year-old son as he could not afford a hotel room, and he didn't have a place to stay. Sometimes, they would take refuge in a church shelter or the bathroom of a subway station. It was amazing that nobody at work knew what he was going through. You see, each morning, when he turned up for work, he would look very passionate about the classes being held. He was enthusiastic and eager to learn, no matter what it took. He made sure that his condition (living in the streets with no money) did not stop him from achieving his dream. In his mind, he was game on. He knew exactly what he wanted, and pursued it relentlessly.

Gardner wanted to be world class at something. When you truly find something that you love, something you want to do every day, if not every minute of the day, you will eagerly share it with the rest of the world with boundless enthusiasm. You will not fear that people will know more than you. Because you know, to teach is to learn twice.

You cannot teach someone how to be passionate about something. They have to be able to identify what they are passionate about. They cannot pretend to be interested in something when they are not. When you are interested or passionate about something, it shows with the amount of energy you exert. It shows in the excitement that you create. Once others see it, you can just feel the positive energy flowing through them and you feel comfortable being next to those people. You can see this energy in their eyes.

When you do something in your life, make sure you are truly committed to it, and never give up, no matter what. Like I often say, once you have set your mind on getting or achieving something that you want badly enough, impossible is no longer a word you will understand or accept.

Identifying Your Desires

Most people don't know exactly what they want. Instead, they are very adept at identifying what they do not want. When people have asked you what you want in life, how many times have you uttered, "I don't want to be like my dad" or maybe when you were younger, "I don't want to go to school" and the likes.

It is equally important to know what you do not want in life as much as what you do want. Only when you have identified what you do not want in life, you will realize and understand the contrast of what you actually want and desire. Think of something that you do not like, do not feel right about, does not feel good or causes you to be and feel negatively about the things around you. By thinking about these negative aspects, negative vibrations are set out in your mind. But by observing contrast and identifying the things you do not want, you gain better clarification and understanding about the things that you do want. The key here is not to sulk about the things you do not want, but merely to identify them.

Imagine you are on your way to dinner with your best mate and he suggests that you have Italian food. But you have already had Italian cuisine twice this week and say you prefer something else. You make some suggestions. He agrees and off you go to a restaurant of your choice. Instantly, you feel much happier and relaxed. This simple example shows how you can become clear about what you want and what you desire by paying attention to what you do not like. In short, your contrast has provided you with clarity of what you do want.

Many a times, we come across things that we do not want to do in life. However, we accept them as a way of life and resign to doing things the same way, with excuses like, "that's just the way things are". Well it does not have to be that way. You decide what you want. In life, you always have a choice. It's whether the choices you make are the right ones. Even if the choices are bad, you can change them into better ones. Once again, you decide.

The key to getting what you want without focusing too much on what you do not want is to understand how long you need to focus on what you do not want. Only you can decide how long a time you need to give yourself. For example, some people may take only a few months to decide whether the person they are dating is the one they want to spend the rest of their lives with. For others, it may take years or perhaps even a lifetime to figure that out! Even though the choices are clear, people lack the courage to make decisions as they are afraid of the abrupt change in their lives.

When you weigh what you do not want in terms of pain, sound, sight or taste, your tolerance level is minimal and you will know almost instantly what you do not want and make a quick decision. This is the clarity we are seeking. For instance, if you put your palm against a boiling kettle, almost immediately you will pull your hand away from it. Likewise, when you hear some annoying music or song on the radio, you will change channels instantly. In these situations, you are absolutely clear on what you do not want and make prompt decisions to change.

There are, however, a few areas in your life in which you have waited longer than you should have. These areas are likely concentrated mostly in relationships, health, career and your finances. You know that the two of you are not meant for each other, but still stay on simply because you are afraid of starting out afresh. You would rather stay stuck in a current relationship than change and hope for something unknown. Take your health for instance. You keep taking puff after puff and tell yourself you will quit next month, or next year or whenever. But you never quit. That's because you delight yourself in instant gratification from what is nice and cozy now rather than discipline yourself into becoming what you know you can. Take another example, your career. You are stuck in your current job but have no courage to plunge into the job market to look for a new job because you are too comfortable with your current role. You have become complacent and refuse to challenge yourself with a new job for fear that it may be worse than your current one.

Generally, these examples, be it pain, sight, career or your relationships, all work in the same way in your subconscious mind as they do in reality. The only difference is in the speed at which you make decisions and the impact they have on your life. Always remember, the less time you spend putting your attention, your energy and focus toward what you do not want, the better. Only when you are clear on what you do not want can you start focusing on what you want in life, with clarity and few doubts.

Pay Attention To Your Desires

Once you have identified what you do want in life with clarity, the next thing you need to focus on is ensuring that you give enough attention to your desire which is to be materialized into reality. Merely identifying your desire and not doing anything to make it a reality will not bring any changes. Many people are good at identifying what they do want. But thereafter, the list of what they want gets slipped into the drawer or wallet, never to be talked about again. Once you have generated a list of what you do want and have a plan on how to manifest it into reality, you need to have a progress report every other day or so, if need be, to ensure that you know where you stand and what needs to be done to keep the list in action.

Once you are absolutely sure of what you do want, you have to learn how to use positive words to give your desire the attention, focus and energy. At this time, there is no doubt that you can achieve this desire you have listed. If you do not believe what you are doing and focusing can be achieved, nobody else will believe it either. Once you sustain that attention, energy and focus on your goals and desires, you will notice a momentum building up and you will be more and more keen on carrying on with what you have started. Spend at least 10-20 minutes daily envisioning that what you want to achieve has already been achieved, what effect and joy it will bring you and how you will feel when you actually achieve it. You need to reaffirm this in your subconscious mind every day until it is no longer a doubt but your reality. This can be done by using what I call positive affirmation. Positive affirmation is a declaration of something which you believe is true. It can be a simple statement or a very complex one such as an oath. Affirmation is a statement spoken in the present tense and used to indicate a desire.

Before you can start using positive affirmative statements, you need to be mindful of a few things. Each time you use an affirmative statement, your physiology and your body language react depending on how the words make you feel. For instance, if you tell yourself that you have a million dollars in the bank, but in actual fact you do not, you are creating a false sense of hope. This will bring more despair and create a negative vibration around you. You will feel depressed, as deep down inside you know you are merely lying to yourself. Initially, I said that for your desires to come true, you need to reaffirm this in a way that you must believe to be true. It must not linger in your subconscious mind as a doubt but your reality. You might then ask, when would I use these affirmations and when will they hold true for me? The key here is when the affirmations are true for you! That's why the words you choose to structure your affirmations are crucial in creating the correct vibrations and impact on how your body responds to these words.

In the previous paragraph, I said that affirmations should be spoken in the present tense. Let us now focus on rewording your affirmations in the form of a "process of becoming", or a "process of doing". That way, it will always hold true for you no matter what affirmations you make. For example if you tell yourself you are in the process of becoming a millionaire, you take steps to ensure it happens, like start a business or something like that. You tell yourself you are in the process of becoming slimmer, fitter and healthier. You take steps to ensure that it happens over time, like cut down on your intake of calories, go to the gym and so forth. You see the difference? When you say you are in the process of becoming or in the process of doing, whatever positive affirmations you make will hold true for you, including any desires you may have while making the affirmations a reality for you. When that happens, you feel better, and it gives you a positive vibration that will impact your subconscious mind in the most remarkable way.

How To Make Positive Affirmations

A simple example of how to make positive affirmation is to have a personal mission statement: something that is your own and yet simple enough for you to be able to achieve. You can also call it your desire statement. Remember, your desire statement must be filled with words that can change your physiology and enable you to have a positive vibration on your subconscious mind. It should have something in the likes of:

- I have decided to ...
- I love having to ...
- I will be a ...
- I love how it feels to ...
- I am in the process of ...

Once you have listed your personal mission statement, you should keep it within easy reach at all times, like your hand phone or your wallet such that you can not go anywhere without them. Limit your affirmations from five to ten main ones so that you can remember them by heart and reaffirm them every morning, afternoon and before you hit the sack at night. You will know that the personal mission statement which you set for yourself is the right one when you read through it and feel a positive vibration going through your mind. You will feel a sort of momentum picking up and a feeling of freshness to start doing things for the better again. If you do not feel that way, most probably, you have written your personal mission statement the wrong way or it is not powerful enough.

Reword your phrases again if you have to, until you get them right. Below are some example personal mission statements to help you on your way:

- I will be committed to ensuring that I live on a healthy diet.
- I love the fact that I will be going to the gym, ensuring that I will live a healthy life, and enjoy the workout every time.
- I enjoy the fact that I will be a self-starting individual who will take the initiative in accomplishing my life's goals and helping others do the same.
- I love the fact that my choice of an ideal partner is someone who understands me for all the things that I am, and is sensitive about my feelings.
- I love the fact that I am in the process of building my courage to challenge myself financially, career-wise as well as emotionally to improve myself as an individual.
- I am grateful for the fact that I am able to learn from my past mistakes, and able to focus on the present situation and prepare for what the future holds for me.

Allowing Your Desires To Take Shape

You have already identified what you desire, and given your desires enough attention. It is time now to allow your desires to happen and make them your reality. You have created your own personal mission statement and have plans on how you are going to get it done. Two of the most powerful sporting brands in the world, *Nike* and *Adidas* have the most powerful and motivating catchphrases: *Just do it* and *Impossible Is Nothing* respectively. These are the two phrases I hold on to whenever I find myself wanting to do something that seems to be beyond my reach. They help carry me through to the point of completion.

Remember that in preceding paragraphs I said that if you have any lingering doubts and send out negative vibrations which will impact your subconscious mind, you are not going to turn any of your desires into reality. Allowing occurs in the absence of doubt. The speed at which you will attain your goals and desires is determined by how much confidence you have that they can be achieved. If you have any doubt, any at all, your goals or desires may come to you slowly, if at all. If you have no doubts, they will come to you at once. You must learn to banish all doubts, however small, before you start to take the next step toward achieving what you have written down.

Described as one of the most powerful men in Malaysian history, Tan Sri Lim Goh Tong can be regarded as one of the movers and pioneers who helped put Malaysia on the world map. However, things did not start out quite well for this Malaysian entrepreneur. Far from it. For those of you who have the limiting belief that you are either too old to start a business, or say that you come from a poor background with no proper financial support or lack support from family and friends, think again.

Here is a story of a man who has defied all odds against him, flirted with death several times, and gone against the advice of many of his friends not to build, I dare say, one of the most legendary tourism spots in Malaysia, if not the world. His dream of building a hilltop resort was completed when he was 52-years-old!

Lim lost his father when he was 16. He then stopped schooling and together with his elder brother, had to work to feed their entire family of five other siblings. Then, he ventured into construction after trying out many other businesses, and even came close to bankruptcy once because of an almost failed project. Lim conceived the idea of building a resort when he was having tea at a hilltop resort in Cameron Highlands. He had a very clear vision of what he wanted to build, and the idea stuck with him and it all became clearer and clearer. As his desire grew stronger each day, so did the resistance and challenges that came his way. All that did not stop him. In fact, it made him all the more determined to carry on.

Pessimists estimated that the time it would take to even build a road up to the hilltop would take around 15 years, but Lim did it in three years! Lim has spent all his life's fortune on building his dream resort and even tried to persuade his close friends and business partners in venturing together with him. But all of them laughed at him. You see, the reason he was so successful was because he knew that he could not fail. He could not afford to fail. If he did, he would lose all that he had worked for so far. Therefore, he overcame challenge after challenge with great perseverance, and only death could keep him from realizing his dream. At last, the dream resort was opened and has become one of the most attractive tourism spots in Asia. At the peak of his career, Lim was the third richest man in Malaysia with an estimated fortune of over $4.2 billion. That is billion with a B!

Never let anyone belittle what dreams you may have, no matter how small or colossal those dreams are. The moment you know you can achieve a dream, that is the moment your dream will manifest itself into reality. To achieve your dream, you need to start by taking a single step, the first step. The rest will naturally follow. It will definitely not be easy, as you will face challenges along the way. Never give up in the face of adversity, and you will see the light at the end of the tunnel.

Desire is merely a word that has no meaning if we do not learn how to let go of the past, focus on the present and prepare for the future. Desire can be a powerful tool if used properly and manifested in our subconscious mind.

Write down the things you don't want	Write down the things you want
Examples:	Examples:
In Health	**In Health**
1. _____	1. _____
2. _____	2. _____
3. _____	3. _____
In Career	**In Career**
1. _____	1. _____
2. _____	2. _____
3. _____	3. _____
In Relationship	**In Relationship**
1. _____	1. _____
2. _____	2. _____
3. _____	3. _____
<u>Acknowledgment</u>	<u>Acknowledgment</u>
Name: _____	Name: _____
Signature: _____	Signature: _____
Date: _____	Date: _____

V
EFFECTIVE LEADERSHIP: THE KEY TO GROWTH AND SUSTAINABILITY

> *"The secret is not in never failing, but to rise each time we fail"*
>
> – Confucius –

Do you remember the sweet little girl called Gertie, from one of the most popular and heart-warming family movies, *The Extraterrestrial* or more widely known as *ET*? This was the girl whose parents were divorced, got entrenched in drug-related activities and went in and out of rehabilitation as a teenager but went on to be one of the most successful actresses in modern time television. Her name is Drew Barrymore, one of the actresses whom I adore.

The talented Barrymore began her acting and modeling career at the tiny age of one year, appearing in one of the commercials for dog food. At 13, she developed an addiction toward drugs and alcohol and had a tendency to be violent. It was reported that the enraged Barrymore once threw her mother out of the house. She regretted the incident and wrote about it in her autobiography entitled *Little Girl Lost.*

After recovering from her addiction, Barrymore went on to secure many successful acting projects that included blockbuster movies such as *Scream, The Wedding Singer* and the successful franchise of *Charlie's Angels.*

Sometimes, when you are down and have nobody to turn to, you often feel that the whole world is against you and everything that you do seems to be wrong. Everyone will go through that period where they start doubting and losing hope that their dream will ever be realized. You can ask any successful person that you know, or google any household names in the fields that you are interested in and all of them will share their stories about times when all odds seem stacked against them. But all of them would have the same advice: Get Up and Try Again.

We often read and hear successful stories of how people have made their millions or how they have achieved their life long goals; but we are never exposed to the work they have put in, the hardships they went through and the sacrifices they have made in order to achieve their dreams. For every goal you pursue, you need to sacrifice something, be it your time, your sleep or any other material thing. It is for you to weigh and prioritize whether sacrificing one thing for another is worth it at the end of the day, when you have achieved what you want.

And know this: it is all right to fall down. It is all right to fail. And it is all right to be wrong sometimes. The main thing is that after you have fallen down, you get up and try again.

I remember when I first started planning for this chapter; I was so excited as I had just finished reading one of the best books on leadership by John C. Maxwell. As I started penning down my first words, my mind was blank. I did not know where to start. There were so many definitions, so many concepts I wanted to try and share. The word leadership alone returns over 160 million results in a Google search!

Many people are often confused with the difference between a manager and a leader. Although both are closely related and have similar traits, they play different roles to move a company in different directions. Managers take care of where you are currently, where leaders take you to new heights. Managers are concerned with doing things right, while leaders are more concerned about doing the right things. Managers see a given situation based on numbers and facts that they have, while leaders see when there is no light, hear when there is no sound. Get the idea?

Good leaders exude influence wherever they go. You will achieve excellence as a leader if your followers follow you wherever you go, even if only just out of curiosity. It is not the position that makes the leader, but the leader that makes the position. A person of power in a high ranking position may have many people under his command, but if he is a bad leader, whatever vision or ideas he shares will not be carried through to his followers. People will not be convinced of his ability to lead them, and thus his influence as a leader can only go so far. Leaders know that in order to grow and move forward, making sacrifices is inevitable. To be an exemplary leader, you have to accept the responsibility and accountability that come with it. It is hard to reach the top. It is even harder to stay there. Have you ever watched the movie *Braveheart?* In that movie, how is it possible for a simple peasant, William Wallace, with no experience in fighting or war, to lead a group of people to freedom? This is because William Wallace, enraged by the killing of his wife, was able to inspire the people to fight with him and thus to win the independence of his country.

Leaders are able to motivate and inspire people into taking action for what needs to be done. They are able to act on limited resources, regardless of how the tide is turning against them. In the Blue Ocean Strategy, W. Chan Kim and Renee Mauborgne shared an interesting concept on motivating employees at work by using the terms and phrases: kingpins, placing these kingpins in a fish bowl and atomization.

Kingpins are people with massive influence in a company. They may have been in the company for years and have a large amount of followers. Much like the first pin in bowling, once you manage to topple it, the other pins will follow suit. These kingpins are well respected, and have persuasive skills to unlock key resources that you may need in order to get a proposal approved, a monthly budget increased and so forth. It is wise to note however, that kingpins may not be the individuals with the highest ranking in the organization. They are just leaders who can influence people to follow their decisions.

Identify your kingpins or key influences in your organization and get them together. This is where the second part of the concept is discussed: placing your kingpins in a fish bowl. When these leaders come together, more often than not, they will be discussing their ideas, vision and missions together. As they are natural leaders, nobody wants to lag behind and get embarrassed. For kingpin management to work, this process must be based on transparency and fair process. Treat all kingpins the same and ensure that everybody knows what the rest are doing. Once all your kingpins start taking action, you will be able to see the incredible ripple effect throughout your organization or department.

In the last section of this concept, it tells of how we can use the idea of atomization to get the organization to change itself. Before any change can be made, all people must first believe that change is attainable. Otherwise, the change is not likely to pull through. That is the key reason why the kingpins play an influential role in getting the ripple effect started. A lot of times when we set seemingly large, impossible goals for ourselves, we tend to give up before we get started on the first item. This is because we fail to break down these goals into achievable goals and to have a game plan on how to achieve them. When you atomize and break down these goals into smaller portions, you will find that these impossible goals are by far attainable. It is much like a jigsaw puzzle: you do the puzzle piece by piece with the bigger picture in your mind.

People in the field of management have been searching for the best style of leadership. However all evidence clearly indicates that there is no single leadership style that works best. Successful leaders are people who can adapt their behavior to meet the demands of a current situation.

The situational leadership model developed by Paul Hersey in the 1960s is based on the amount of direction a leader must provide, given a situation and the readiness of the followers or group. Look at the table below:

Participating	Selling
• Low direction • High support Leaders share ideas and facilitate in making decisions.	• High direction • High support I will decide, we will talk. Explain your decisions, but provide opportunity for clarification.
Delegating	Telling
• Low direction • Low support You will decide, I will be available.	• High Direction • Low support I will decide and tell you what to do.

In Participating, leaders often communicate what needs to be done to the followers. Although the leaders are there to give ideas and support, however, the main decisions lie in the hands of the followers. This type of leadership is suitable for followers and staff who are more mature.

In Selling, leaders make decisions but provide opportunity to their staff to clarify why they have taken such a step. Ultimately the decision still stands. This type of leadership is often applied for staff who are still new and need clear directions and expectations of what to do. This is where the leaders need to explain and clarify why they have made certain decisions.

Delegating, from my point of view, is the most sensitive kind of leadership as it provides low direction as well as low support to the followers. If not used properly, it will cause followers to have low morale and potentially disrupt the trust that employees have in their managers. In this aspect, the leaders are still involved in the decision-making and the problem solving, but the followers will decide when and how the leaders should be involved. It gives the most empowerment to the employees to decide what they think is right and must be done. This part of leadership style is most suitably used where there is a project to be completed. Once autonomy has been given to the employees or staff concerned, they can pretty much decide how to run or complete the project.

Telling leadership style is considered by many as one of the most rigid leadership styles, where leaders provide specific instructions and closely supervise the performance. In this instance, leaders define the tasks, roles and responsibilities of the followers. Decisions are usually made by the leaders and communication is mostly one way traffic. This style of leadership is mostly suitable for staff who have low competency and maturity as they need clear instructions on how to do certain tasks. If left unsupervised, they may leave you in a lurch wondering if it is better to do those tasks yourself.

Which type of leadership style you implement will largely depend on the type of followers. If your staffs are largely independent and can work on their own and if you start micro managing them and directing them on how you want them to do what you think is right, you will find that their productivity can be affected and their performance will drop.

Managers must realize that although employees are motivated, highly skilled and confident in their tasks, their competency level may drop when faced with an unfamiliar task requiring skills they do not possess. Imagine you were an employee whose daily tasks and responsibilities are arranging meetings and answering calls. All of a sudden, the computer breaks down and your boss expects you to fix it in two hours. You start to panic, not knowing what to do. Your productivity goes haywire and when your boss comes back after two hours, he is going to be angry. Good leaders get the right person for the right job. The logic is simple. I am sure you are not going to get your dentist to advise you on how to repair your door. Much like you are not going to ask a truck driver how to perform an operation. You find the right person for the job.

The Vision Of The Leader

Have you ever been struck by someone so hard that it has made it almost impossible to get up again? It may not have been a physical blow, but a psychological blow from someone that you trusted. Someone who betrayed your trust and did things that you never thought possible. It would be worse if you were right on top in your field and you may even wonder if you would get up again.

When we are slapped in the face or faced with a daunting challenge, when our critics hit us hard, we sometimes forget that the simplest support we can get is from people that love us, people that care about us, people that demand nothing more from us, but merely our presence. It is with them that we are able to come back stronger, wiser and more committed to fight the cause that we believe in. And remember, regret comes when we have not learned from our experience.

A vision is the ability to see what others cannot. It requires the willpower to act upon that vision to make it a reality. People will follow your vision when they trust you. The greatest example is Adolf Hitler. He was a very intelligent man but with a crooked vision; he was able to buy into the masses of people to follow him and do what he wanted. If you are a leader with integrity, that is enough reason for others to put their faith in you. Then they will buy into your vision, the place you want to take them. No matter how worthy or how pure visions seems to be, people will only follow leaders who promote worthwhile causes.

Bear in mind that as a leader, each of your steps is scrutinized. Everything you do, takes great mention as people strive to emulate you. You need to lead by example. When you do that, you do not have to set the rules on what is right or wrong. For instance, if you keep telling your children that smoking is bad for their health, and they see you, their father puffing away with a cigarette in his mouth, how do you think your children are going to take that message? Keep it simple. Walk the talk. Do what you say you are going to do.

You are the message. Every message, every meaning or perspective that people perceive through their eyes is filtered through their belief system. If you truly believe the person sending the message is trustworthy, then automatically the message which that person conveys has value. Why do sports companies pay millions to icons like Ronaldinho, Michael Jordan or even Tiger Woods to advertise their products? It is because the public sees these people as role models in their everyday lives, achieving what is possible.

Whatever message these sporting icons send out is credible and has value. When the advertisement is repeated over and over again, it reinforces the message into your belief system. The next time you see a product, you will relate it with the message that is being conveyed by these superstars.

As a leader, you do not get credit or earn any brownie points for being right. Your success is measured by your ability to take your people to where they NEED to go, not where they THINK they must go. You can only do so if your followers first buy into you as a leader.

The Art Of Persuasion

Have you ever been to a flea market? It is place where vendors congregate to sell or trade their goods. There are probably hundreds of vendors trying to persuade you to buy their goods. Why is it that sometimes two stalls offer identical products at different prices and some buyers might opt for the more expensive one? This is because some vendors use the art of persuasion and activate what I would like to call "meta programs". To be able to effectively persuade your subordinates to undertake certain responsibilities or to propose a new idea to your superior, you need to know what meta programs are running on.

Meta programs are mental processes which manage, guide and direct other mental processes. These are the programs that make you decide why you had decided to take the left turn today on your way to work rather than following the normal route. Different people, depending on their internal representation or their frame of reference, have one dominant program that runs their decision making every single day.

The first common meta program everybody uses, consciously or otherwise, is our "moving toward" or "moving away" values. Some people move toward something, others move away. To find out in which direction they are moving, ask them what they want in a relationship, what their goals are, about their jobs or anything else. You will be able to gather some information on their direction.

Everybody moves in unison, whether toward a goal or away from pain. You pull away from a boiling kettle to avoid being scalded. You sit down with your friend and have dinner at an exquisite restaurant because you get pleasure from relaxation and the cuisine served. This is true for our other actions. You ride the bicycle to work because you enjoy the exercise or you do it simply because you are afraid to drive. When your boss gives you certain responsibilities with a tight deadline, you work extra hours because you enjoy and relish the challenge given or you do it because you want to avoid being reprimanded. Everyone moves toward or away, to a certain extent. Each person has a dominant mode.

When this information is evident, you can use it to your advantage. For instance, when a sales person sells a service or a product, he can promote it in two ways: by presenting what it does and what it does not do. If you are selling a phone, you promote the many features of the phone and how far it can call. You can also promote how it does not often break down, does not take much time to maintain and does not cost much. Your selling point or method that you use depends on who you are selling to. If that person is a "moving toward" person but you keep on selling to him using a "moving away" method such as how it does not cost much or does not often break down, chances are he is going to the next stall to look for better options.

Similarly, parents who want their children to get a good education need to understand what programs their children are running on. If your child is running on a "moving away" program, telling him to study hard so that he can get into a good college is not going to motivate him to ace his exams. You may want to try something like this, "Honey, you need to study hard so that you do not have to spend half your life waiting at tables". Give him something to move away from. If he is motivated by things that are exciting, say something like, "Son, you need to study hard so that you can get a scholarship and go anywhere you want to go". Do not just take my word that this strategy works. Observe the people around you. Your colleagues, your friends and even your family. Practise it now. Ask questions to find out what their meta programs are. You will notice how effectively they will respond if you use the right key.

The next major meta program deals with internal and external stimulus. Are there times when you feel absolutely incredible? Have you ever wondered why? Is it because you have been praised by your boss for doing a great job? Or is it because you know YOU did a good job deep down inside? Do you feel good because of an internal incident or external frame of reference?

If you are feeling great because your boss or your friend has praised you for something you did right, then you are most probably sorted by an external frame of reference. You know you have done well when you get a nod of approval from an external factor and that is referred to as an *external frame of reference*. For others, the proof may come from inside. When they have completed a task after spending countless hours and much effort, they feel an inner satisfaction and are confident that they have done well. Likewise, if you receive heaps of praise from people around you but you know that you did not put much effort in the project, no amount of external awards can give you the satisfaction you want and need. You trust your instincts more than you trust others.

When you try to convince your friend to go to a new restaurant, you can use either way, depending on his frame of reference. If he sorts externally, you may say, "You have to check out this restaurant, all our friends have gone, and everybody says it has great food. Even John, who is so fussy about food, agrees!" If everybody, especially his friends, agrees that the restaurant serves great food, he will probably follow you to the restaurant. But if he sorts internally, you will have a difficult time convincing him as he already has a definition of what a good restaurant means to him. You may want to link him to his past experiences with great restaurants by appealing to things he knows himself. You can say something like, "Remember the place we went last time, which you said was fantastic? Well there is this place where the environment is similar and you might enjoy it as well. If you check it out, you may find a similar experience at this new place". I guarantee you that it will work because you are speaking his language.

However, it is important to note that if you have already done certain things for ages, although you can change your frame of reference, most likely you have a strong and rigid internal frame of reference. This is because you have already done something so many times and experience has convinced you that this is what will happen if you do it this way. If someone else tells you something different, you know based on experience that it is not so, and hence will not be easily convinced. But if you are brand new, you will be easily swayed by hearsay and other people's opinions. It is important to know that you can vary and change.

Effective leaders have strong internal frames of reference. This is because they need to make tough decisions based on what they feel is correct, internally. They cannot be effective leaders if they spend most of their time asking people's opinions on what they feel would be the best decision. But a balance of both internal and external frames of reference is required to run or manage a team effectively.

The next factor that influences a decision depends on whether the individual is sorted by self or others. You might have already realized that people around you may do things for themselves or may sacrifice their time for others. Some of us look at daily interactions with people in terms of what is beneficial for "me", while some of us may look at things in a more altruistic manner. A person may lean towards one extreme or the other, but never 100% skewed to one side. If you were sorted by self all of the time, you would probably be a selfish, egotistic person that nobody would want to have anything to do with. And if you were sorted by others all the time, people may start taking advantage of you, leaving you helpless and on the losing end.

The next question you may ask is, "If I were a business person, what sort of employees would I want on my payroll?" That depends if you are in the service line or customer service. If you hired someone sorted by self, the person would be most self-conscious of what he would be getting and what he could do for himself rather than for his fellow colleagues or clients he is servicing. You would be looking for candidates sorted by others so that they would know what they could do for others, not what they could do for themselves. In the service industry, you need to tell the customers what YOU CAN DO for them, not what you cannot do! Although the answer is the same, the impact is different. Notice the sentences below and the way they are phrased:

> Mr. John, you will only be eligible to enjoy
> the free gifts after 1 year with us.

> **As opposed to:**

> Mr. John, you are not eligible to enjoy the free
> gifts as your membership has not reached 1 year.

> Mr. Customer, you can buy this customized software
> if your purchases within a single receipt reach $200.

> **As opposed to:**

> Mr. Customer, you are not eligible to purchase this
> customized software as your purchases are less than
> $200.

Get the idea? The trick is to identify types of people who are sorted by self as well as others. To help determine this, notice the amount of attention they give to others. Does a person show genuine concern towards what the other party is saying? Or does he show a lack of respect when others are talking? In a given situation, do they give you the best answers which only benefit themselves? Are they more concerned with how they can avoid trouble or are they concerned with the general welfare of the group? The key is finding the right balance which group the person belongs to to produce the results that you desire most and finally towards achieving what they want.

The last major meta process involves similarity and differences. People who fall into this category are called "matchers" and "mismatchers". Matchers are people who look for things which are similar, which have some common agenda, while mismatchers always tend to look at how things are different or how things can go against them. Both are equally important if used at the right time. Any ideas or plans that I concoct and conjure up, I tend to think of what could go wrong and how to find a workaround before the ideas actually take off. Most people tend to look at this as pessimism. Far from it. Initially, when my friends and I sat down together to brainstorm certain ideas, they would tend to get frustrated as every conceivable idea would be shot down by what I perceived to be possible or potential operational issues. Once, we got so frustrated that I promised I would keep quiet and agree only should the majority agree. After several months using the idea, issues started arising. Again we sat down (with me in commanding charge this time) to brainstorm on what else could possibly go wrong and how to find viable solutions. You see, it is not about looking at the negative point of view only, but being able to come up with an idea that counters that thought or to find a workaround to that negative idea; this is what makes a pessimist different from a mismatcher. However, mismatchers are in the minority as they are always finding differences in people. Matchers are able to easily develop rapport with others.

To determine whether a person is a "sameness" type or a "difference" type test him on the relationship between a set of objects and notice whether the person sees what the objects have in common or what is different between them. The next question is, can a matcher and a mismatcher live together? Can they work as partners on a multimillion dollar project? Sure they can. As long as both parties understand each other when differences occur, one person is not right or wrong, but just perceives things differently from another. Beware that each person perceives things from a different perspective and try to learn to respect and appreciate the opinions and views of others. Someone once said, "Try to see things from the other person's perspective sometimes, and you may see that the sky is a different blue".

Values

What are values? Or more importantly, what type of values should leaders have? What drives leaders to have the values that they need? Values are drivers that move us toward or away from certain tasks, decisions that affect our everyday lives, from meager issues like choosing our favourite toothpaste to calling on that cold lead to make the $10,000 deal. If you ask any leader in any field, you will notice that each has a number one value that they live by and breathe diligently to their core routine every single day.

When World War II ended, there was a time of political instability, and the black and white people were segregated in every aspect of their daily lives in the south, including public transportation. Bus and train companies did not provide separate vehicles for the different races but enforced seating policies that allocated separate sections for blacks and whites. School buses took white students to their schools while black students had to walk to theirs. Mixed marriages between blacks and whites were virtually unheard of.

The courage of one woman changed all that just by the simple act of determination. She refused to give up her seat to a white man on a bus where the black and white people were segregated. Rosa Louise McCauley Parks said, "When that white driver stepped back toward us, I felt a determination cover my body like a quilt on a winter night". The driver had her arrested, which sparked a nationwide movement and she became an icon of the civil rights movement.

Parks knew that the values she had in her were the inner force that kept her going till the very end. It kept her feet on the ground when everybody was against her. She was an ordinary person with extraordinary determination. You do not have to be blessed with a special talent. You do not have to know anyone special. Nor do you need to be faster, taller, bigger or better. To do what is right, you just need to have the will and determination to follow through whenever the going gets tough.

When everyone and all odds seem stacked against you, do not give up too soon. It may take years before you achieve anything worthwhile. But know this: all great things begin with a single step. You can achieve anything you want if you are determined not to be knocked down by people who could be jealous of what you want to achieve.

Your critics will always try to find faults with you. That is their job. If you did not have critics, you would never know where to improve yourself. Your job is to make their lives difficult by doing the best you know you can do.

I mentioned earlier that everybody moves toward or away from something. It is the same with values. Some individuals have "away" values, while some have "toward" values. You must know what your "toward" and "away" values are. From there you will learn how to prioritize your values to work for you, instead of against you. For instance, some people value success more than love. An individual may work late night shifts, go for double jobs and spend a great deal of time at work in order to climb the corporate ladder while his loved ones are waiting at home. This is because on his ladder of values, success comes before love. Therefore, he is willing to sacrifice what he defines as love for success. For some, friendship comes before money. An individual may be willing to be a guarantor for his best friend in a risky business venture as long as he trusts enough the value of the friendship. This is because on this guy's ladder values, monetary terms become secondary compared to a friend in need. While for others, it may be freedom before a relationship. If an individual is asked by his girlfriend to report every hour on his whereabouts, you can be sure that the relationship will not last long. How you sort your values will determine what values you hold closest to your heart. Below are examples of some "toward" and "away" values:

TOWARD	AWAY
• Love	• Rejection
• Success	• Embarrassment
• Happiness	• Failure
• Freedom	• Fear
• Relationship	• Frustration
• Security	• Loss
• Responsibility	• Guilt
• Accountability	
• Integrity	

In order to discover what your "toward" values are, you will need to ask three main questions:

What is most important in your life? In other words, what do you value most in your life? Is it pride? Personal achievement? Recognition? Happiness? Sense of accountability? Fame? Freedom? You must be as specific as possible. Bear in mind that these must be values and not objects like a house or property or money. If you say, "I value my $2 million-dollar house above everything else", then ask what does owning the house give you? Sense of achievement? Pride?

Next, go back to a period when you were in a most effective state, a time when you were able to get a lot of things done in the shortest time possible. Visualize yourself in that time again and ask what made you so motivated and energetic? Why were you in such a good mood? What were the emotional states that were attached to that situation?

Was it satisfaction? Pride? Recognition? Fame? Sense of achievement? Again, be as specific as possible.

Lastly, and this is the most important question, how do you know when you have achieved the values that you have specified? What must happen before you feel valued? Many people fail to recognize their achievements or their goals when they have reached them and therefore, they end up feeling miserable and frustrated after working so hard and not being able to reap the benefits. Once all those values are listed down specifically, such as sense of achievement and pride, ask what needs to be done for you to feel proud of yourself. What do you need to feel that you have achieved something? You cannot just think about it, you must write it down specifically, and keep referring to it until you know it by heart. People are only motivated to work if they know what they are aiming for.

As much as I would like to continue talking about "toward" values, "away" values are also part and parcel of our lives, which we need to be aware of and are every bit as important. What are your "away" values? Rejection? Embarrassment? Failure? And what must happen for you to feel this way? Do you feel rejected when someone turns you down for a dinner date? Or when you get laughed at in the middle of a presentation? List down all the possible values that you have which may cause you to move away from something.

Once you have listed these values down, compare them with the "toward" values that were listed earlier. Put them in front of you and see whether the decisions you have previously made have been affected by those values. Do these values explain why you have made those decisions in your relationships, in your personal life, in your career, personal development? Do you find that when you are in conflict, the values you rank upper most in your hierarchy of values tend to be involved when you make the final call? Take as much time as you need to sort this out.

Once this is sorted out, understand that you can make positive changes to these values and their rankings. You can control which rank first, second and so on. How do you do that? Firstly, you must understand that the core values change whenever we encounter significant life-changing experiences which affect our lives directly. For instance, you were almost robbed at knife point while taking the LRT today, or you have just had your first born after a few years of trying. Respectively, safety will be your first value and family top priority.

I have a friend who used to like late night partying, booze and high-end adventures, until he was diagnosed with liver failure. Before, his number one value was fun. After the diagnosis, he began to shift his values. He placed health as his top priority value and as of now, with me writing this book, he is working out in the gym and is currently in top shape. Keep this in mind however, not everyone gets a second chance in life.

After you have listed down all your values from one to ten and you would like to change them, find ways to integrate your new values so that your subconscious mind will start to strengthen the belief that the new values will actually benefit you. In time, your conscious mind will follow suit and these new values will soon be habit. Remember, motivation is what gets you started, habit is what keeps you going.

In summary, if you want to integrate new values into your life, you need to emotionally link these values with all the benefits that you will achieve by having these values. Use the power of visualization to see yourself doing things and making decisions based on these new values and beliefs you have decided to be your top ranking generals. With constant practice, when the time comes or when you reach a T-junction and you need to make a choice, be sure that the decision you make will be based on the new value that you have locked as the top ranking value. As such, there will not be any conflict of interests.

VI

RELATIONSHIPS, TEAMWORK AND YOU

> "Alone we can do
> so little, together
> we can achieve
> so much"
>
> – Helen Keller –

Let us now reflect on how much a single individual can contribute to a cause, whether his contribution is significant enough to have the desired impact. How important is teamwork, and within teamwork, what are the relationships involved to make teamwork a success? We often hear that teamwork is fundamental in a successful organization. Can all work be done on an individual basis? If not, why? We also hear that two heads are better than one, etc. But in fact, how does teamwork operate? What makes a winning team? Why do some teams go straight to the top, winning title after title while some seem to languish in the bottom half?

What is the definition of teamwork? Teamwork is the concept of a team, working together, hand in hand and cooperatively, such as a sports team. Projects that require more than one person can be called team projects. A team's purpose is to group people to achieve a common goal. To achieve anything you want in your life, be it a financial goal, an emotional attachment, your life's purpose or even your spiritual goal, we need people around to push us, to give us a little nudge every now and then, to encourage us forward, to cause conflicts, yes you heard me, to cause conflicts in order to set our mind to thinking.

Even people who have worked in a team for most of their lives find it hard to differentiate between what makes a winning team from a group of mediocre individuals. These people have run out of ideas and as a result, their team loses sight of the common purpose, the common goal. Results plummet and losses soar. We often read news of some coach who has been with a club for years, who suddenly gets sacked, simply because his team cannot perform or garner the result they desire. It is all too common when the same approach is used over and over again and the team lacks freshness. Individuals win games, teams win championships. Legendary football figures like Maradona and Pele have taken the game of football to another level with their mesmerizing ball tricks and skills, but they could have never done it without the support of their coach, their teams and of course, their fans.

With a clear understanding of what a team is and what it takes to achieve team success, we can now identify what it takes to get a team started on the right foot. To build an effective team, there are many aspects we must take a look at

> "There are no problems we cannot solve together, and very few that we can solve by ourselves"
> – Lyndon Johnson –

– the role of a leader, the role of the team members, characteristics of each team member, conflicts within a team and how to solve them, team development, how to achieve motivation in team building activities and many more.

As the challenge unfolds, the need for teamwork also increases to a substantial level. People have tried to scale the highest and the deepest as a measure of their achievements. Back in the early 1900s, people have tried to scale Mount Everest, but to no avail. For 32 years, between 1920 and 1952, numerous expeditions tried and failed to make it to the top of Everest, resulting in the deaths of some of the worlds most renowned mountain climbers.

To achieve a feat of such magnitude, a great amount of teamwork is needed. Tenzing Norgay, the Sherpa who accompanied the first man ever to have scaled Mount Everest, remarked, "You do not climb a mountain like Everest by trying to race ahead on your own, or by competing with your comrades. You do it slowly and carefully, by unselfish teamwork. I certainly wanted to reach the top myself, it was the thing I had dreamed of all my life. But if the lot fell to someone else, I would take it like a man, and not a cry-baby. For that is the mountain way".

On 29th May 1953, Sir Edmund Hillary and Tenzing Norgay accomplished what no other human had: they reached the summit of Mount Everest. Do you think Hillary could have done it on his own? Or Norgay? Or maybe just the two of them together? The answer is a definite no. This is because to accomplish a task of such magnitude would require great amount of teamwork, training and perseverance, among other things.

You may not be interested in climbing Mount Everest but I am sure that you have a dream. Surely everybody has a dream. You may not know it yet or it may be in a blurry sketch of unclear images. But if you have a dream, you need a team to accomplish it.

And when you dream of accomplishing something great, make sure that your team is the size of your dream. John C. Maxwell says it best in his book, *The 17 Indisputable Laws of Teamwork*, "You simply cannot achieve an ultimate number ten dream with a number four team. It just does not happen. It is better to have a great team with a weak dream than a great dream with a weak team".

When your team measures up to the size of your dream, this is the time when you will notice great things start to happen. All the goals and the planning that the team has done will start to materialize. The work rate, cohesiveness and motivation will be automatic of course, provided you have a significant leader who will sacrifice for the good of the team.

When you are in a team, whether it is a small or big team, it does not grow, improve and reach championship caliber all on its own. In order for each team to reach the next level, it must have catalysts. Catalysts are key people that make things happen in a team. Winning teams have players who make things happen.

I am a great enthusiast of soccer. The team I admire most is Liverpool FC. On that team, they have players who make things happen. This is one of the reasons why they reached the final of the Champions League, the most prestigious soccer competition in Europe twice in the last three years. And they have been the European champions an unprecedented five times in their history. This team just does not know when to get beaten.

Their captain, Steven Gerrard, who has a "never say die" attitude, motivates his players when they are losing and more often than not, comes up with the winning goal in crucial times when they are trailing behind the opponents. In 2005, when they were contesting the Champions League final in Istanbul, Turkey, they were lagging behind AC Milan by three goals to nil at half time. Every one in the world thought they were finished and the trophy would go to Italy. Then, when the referee blew the whistle for the second half to start, they came back with a renewed spirit and determination to claw back into the game. They knew even if they lost, they needed to give their fans something to cheer about.

In six and a half amazing minutes, they were level, three all. Their opponents were stunned. The whole world could not believe their eyes. And they fought their way into the extra time and won in the penalties. It was indeed a miracle to see them come back from the dead.

And a year later, contesting in the FA Cup final, trailing three goals to two in the final minutes, their captain marvel, Steven Gerrard, blasted in a goal from 35 yards to earn his side a draw. They fought through the extra time, and won again in penalties.

Winning teams have an aura around them that other teams do not. They just cannot accept the word defeat until it is over. Their sense of determination and confidence are second to none. And most important of all, they have individuals who make things happen. Although it is true that individuals win games and teams win championships, but it is individuals who make things happen, change the course of a game from a losing one to a winning one, and switch strategy from defence to offence.

The same applies to any other team. If you want to build a winning team, make sure you have catalysts that make things happen.

The Role Of The Team Leader

As we mentioned earlier, a team is a group of people focused on one common goal, one common purpose. All teams must have a leader, an individual that can bind a team together. If there are differences of opinion, the leader must assess the information that he has and make a final judgement. There can rarely be two leaders in a team. Likewise, there can only be one captain that steers the ship. Otherwise, a team member may become confused of the direction and whom he has to follow. If there is no clear leadership, members of a team lose direction, and lose focus on the common goal. Conflicts become common ground and motivation will be at an all time low. You may have already experienced this in your workplace where teams are not properly segregated and the company's vision and mission are not clearly defined by the leaders.

When selecting a team leader for a group assignment, the chosen individual must stand out among his fellow colleagues as a leader. Teams expect their leaders to use common sense and analyze from vantage point to help the teams clarify and commit to their mission, goals and approach. Vantage point is the position that offers one a broad overall view or a perspective, of a place or a situation. He should be able to see things from many different angles when making a decision, which must be for the good of the team, for the common purpose which is shared as a group. He must be selfless enough to be able to make that call, and be decisive when the time comes. More often than not, he must be able to make tough calls in a split second and not hesitate. That is why the team leader is accountable for the actions of his team members.

In a battle, when the commanding officer instructs his fellow men to do certain tasks, these tasks are to be obeyed without any question or doubt. When doubts linger, lives are at stake and battles may be lost in a moment of indecisiveness.

A strong team leader must have a significant presence amongst his members. He must be able to keep the purpose, goals and approach relevant and meaningful. Sometimes, teams set goals that are too far-fetched and unattainable with the current resources. Over time, when members keep working on that seemingly unattainable goal, resources become too stretched out, while team members get burned out and demotivated. When this happens, the team leader may want to reassess his team's goals and realign them to work best according to his team's strengths and weaknesses. The leader may be required to break down these goals into smaller pieces and assign them to appropriate members who are deemed fit to accomplish the given tasks. Once these smaller tasks are complete, the leader must be able to acknowledge the fact that the team members have successfully completed a string of tasks together. This will in turn build up enough confidence for the rest of the members to carry out other, more Herculean tasks.

Team leaders protect their teams from outside hazards that threaten to harm the unity of the team. These threats may also come from within. This is where the team leader must be able to assess and manage the relationships among the team members and create a harmonious environment in which everybody pulls their own weight. Potential obstacles that may hinder or threaten the effort that the team has already put through, or which might demoralize the team, must be removed. Mutual trust among teammates is crucial and critical to a team's success. This begins with the leader who must show the team that they can depend on him to promote team performance. Like it's always been said, teamwork is born when people concentrate on WE instead of ME. Cooperation is spelt as W-E. Working together means winning together.

Reasons Why People Refuse
To Work In A Team

There are several reasons why some people refuse to work as part of a team and prefer to work on an individual basis. The main reason is ego. Few people are ready to admit that they cannot do everything. They want to impress their boss by saying they can undertake all the responsibilities thrown at them. But the more responsibilities they take, the sooner they realize that they cannot cope. Andrew Carnegie said it well when he opined "It marks a big step in your development when you come to realize that other people can help you do a better job that you could do alone". To achieve something great, let go of your ego, and get ready to be a part of a team.

The second possible reason why some people refuse to work in a team is insecurity. They find that being in a team may expose their weaknesses or people may tend to compare them with other members from the same team. Leaders who are insecure fail to build strong teams because two possible reasons: they are afraid that giving too much control to the team may supersede their own power, or they could be replaced by someone more capable. These insecure leaders want to maintain control over everything for which they are responsible. These leaders who fail to promote teamwork only undermine the team's effort and magnify their own weaknesses.

Characteristics Of Effective Teams

Everyone in a team needs to be crystal clear about their tasks and responsibilities and the role he or she needs to undertake to be an effective team player. What makes an effective team? There are some key characteristics that significantly define one team from another, be it the style of engaging in some of the assigned tasks or responsibilities, or any common landmark or logo that sets them apart.

One of the most essential characteristics of an effective team is having a clearly defined goal and plan. Each team member must know why he is assigned a specific role or responsibility and has to have a clear cut idea of how to achieve that goal. If not, the member must know where to find or elicit that information in order to be effective. Otherwise, there may be a gaping hole in the team and by the time the leader finds out, he may already be behind schedule or the goal in its entirety may not be achieved within the time frame set. It is imperative that leaders keep track of the tasks and goals that each member is assigned to, and as soon as one of them hits a wall, he or she knows where to find the support needed to pull through.

A second characteristic of an effective team is 100% commitment to the team's goals and objectives by all members of a team. When each member is fully committed to the task at hand, he is willing to go the extra mile to exceed the expectations of their team leaders and their existing goals. More often than not, there are members who do just the minimum to survive in a team, hoping that their minimal contribution will help them pull through whatever necessary performance is required of them. If this is not checked properly, this member will seep morale from the team and bring conflict among members.

The next characteristics that define an effective team are responsibilities and contributions. This is when the team leaders map out clearly defined roles, goals and responsibilities to each member of the team to ensure that each active member is contributing fairly their share of the task. If the leader does not clearly define goals and roles, collectively and individually, the team will eventually feel lost, not knowing what they are contributing toward, unsure of their team's direction, and when this happens, the team's morale and productivity will plummet.

Another characteristic worth mentioning is interpersonal relationships. Between members of any team, be it an organization, a football team, or a team of rugby players, respect for each other must be observed, regardless of age, skin colour, religion, background and so forth. The movie *Remember the Titans* by Denzel Washington is an inspirational movie about teamwork and how to get the best from each individual on the team, regardless of race. In this movie, the football players have to learn how to work together with people from a different race, background and talent. When a common purpose is put together with enough conviction and perseverance, anything is possible.

You are in a team for a common purpose, be it to achieve a common goal set forth by the team leader or to achieve a target that has been clearly defined. Individual talent, as important as it is, will not be able to achieve what teams can achieve. Individuals win matches, teams win championships. We have heard how sporting teams that have internal conflicts crash out of team competitions. In-house-fighting among board members over team decisions, team leaders and managers, brings uncertainty. When this happens, individuals among the team lack trust and faith. Negative attitude surrounds each individual, and the results will soon show in a negative light.

Of course, any team with a lack of leadership will not go far. Therefore the next important characteristic is strong leadership and decisiveness. For a team to move forward, the team has to have clear goals and responsibilities. But who is more appropriate than the team leader to map out these goals clearly to its team members? The leader has to guide individuals into fulfilling their duties in the team and has to effectively manage the team so that motivation can remain high for a goal to be accomplished. If the leader is not decisive enough, more often than not, he will lose the confidence of fellow team members. The leader must take responsibility for his decisions, be they good or bad. He must be accountable for all the team's objectives and goals and answerable to any of the team's shortcomings. Therefore, in order to have a strong team, you need to pick a strong leader who understands the fundamentals of a team, team members' roles and responsibilities.

Identity Identifies Your Team

A team that is strong and cohesive shares a common identity, something that binds the members together, a common resemblance, similar to how a son has his father's good looks or how a daughter has her mother's blue eyes. Each team has its own identity that is different and unique from the other teams. Shared values identify and define the team.

Sometimes, some members of a team may not share common experience, may not have a personal relationship with other members, or may not share a common ground and cohesiveness that defies the size of the team. If everyone embraces the same values, team members can still have a connection to one another and to the larger cause of the team. We often see teams which lack common purpose and values, and when everyone wants to instill his own ideas into the team, the result is chaos. Eventually the team breaks down if everyone wants to do things their way. There cannot be two captains steering a ship.

Just how individual values shape a person, organizational values are just as important to bring the company forward with core values which everybody can relate to.

A team's values serve as an attraction for like-minded people who share the same ideas and values in that team. When you form a swimming club, a political party or a rock band, each group has a common purpose: the swimming club to teach its members how to swim and maybe win competitions; the political party to fight for the injustice it feels is getting worse; the rock band to make music and come up with their own album. Who you are is who you attract. People attract other like-minded people. Birds of a feather flock together.

Strong values also set the basic foundation for people in a team to grow and further progress in their careers and lives. This is true for any relationship to grow to the next level. For example, if you are building a relationship with an individual from a different background and culture, you would first look into the things that you both have in common and strike out a conversation. Only if the relationship goes to the next level, will you start to see differences in opinions. This is when a compromise takes place so that each can understand the other's point of view and thus grow from there. The same can be said for team building. You need strong and basic values to build on what you currently have to take the team to the next level.

When the going gets tough, I believe that right values are what hold the team together. Take a partnership for example. It is easy for young entrepreneurs to venture into something new and exciting and to dream of earning millions of dollars and retire young. When they start up, they are bustling with confidence and enthusiasm. But if partners do not set the correct expectations and the right foundation for who is in charge of what and when to compromise, or who makes what decisions in time of conflict, each partner feels that they are making the right decision. Adversity thrives. What can keep the partnership together? What can hold their friendship through the ultimate test? It is their values, their vision and the individuals' willingness to cling to the belief of those values.

If these individuals highly value their partnership and friendship, they are willing to fight for the success of the partnership. Otherwise, their chances of staying friends are slimmer than slim. The same is true for any other partnership to thrive, be it in a normal working team or in a marriage. The set of individuals must have predetermined values which they live by and believe in. Otherwise, their chances of working together as a cohesive unit and growing as a team are very small, to say the least.

Sport is one of the activities in which teamwork plays a vital role in ensuring whether the team succeeds or fails. As with all teams, each has their own star players with certain values; people who make things happen with their unique understanding of the game, people who are willing to sacrifice for the good of the team.

One of the greatest individuals in the team game is Michael Jordan, the greatest player to have ever touched the game of basketball. He has won two Olympic gold medals, six NBA world championships, has been named NBA's MVP five times and holds numerous records that have yet to be broken.

He is an amazing individual that makes things happen, by simply being him. There is no introduction needed. Whenever his team needed to get out of a bad patch, they would rely on him. Whenever they needed to take the last shot of a game in which they were trailing by a couple of points, they would pass the ball to him. Even in practice, they would be more motivated if he was there for the team. Their team knows that no matter where the wind blows, they can rely on him to make things happen, to get them to their destination. Winning teams have special individuals who make things happen. These people are influential, reliable and responsible.

As long as you are in a team, whether in sports or life, you need people to make things happen. Without these people, it is like a ship without a captain. Although the team has specific goals, the goals may take longer to achieve when sailing without a captain.

These individuals or catalysts have certain attributes or values that make them unique. Among the most important characteristics is good communication with people. They are able to inspire their team when it needs a timely boost. They can get their message across.

Not only that, but catalysts are also passionate about the field they are currently in. They do not need to be pushed. They automatically push themselves to the next level. When you are passionate about something, you constantly find ways to improve yourself in that respect. Nobody should have to tell you to do this or that. You run on auto mode. The passion often spills over to the rest of the teammates as a dose of inspiration and motivation.

Four Simple Ways To Achieve
Effective Teamwork

There are countless ways to lead a team, or to get more out of your existing team. The key is to find out what works best for individual members. Some may respond better to a certain way while others may need more time before adapting to a team leader's assessment and methodology. I would like to share with you four basic ways to achieve greater teamwork and accountability among team members and how to assist them to achieve their goals and targets.

1. **Stay focused on the goal and your team no matter what.**

   After the team leader has clearly defined the team's goals and objectives, it is vital to remind all individuals that when they are pursuing their goal, it is common to meet challenges that may make the entire goal seemingly impossible. It is during these times that the team leader must give enough support to his members so that each individual is clearly focused on the task at hand and doesn't lose sight of the common purpose which the team was set up with in the first place. My ex-boss used to tell us to focus on our people, and the goal will take care of itself. I did not realize the importance of this until later when I had a team of my own. Most people make the common mistake of staying focused on the goal, but neglecting their team in the process. Regardless of how big your dreams or goals are, if you fail to focus on your people, your dreams will falter and collapse. But if you build the right team with the right people, the dreams and goals will almost take care of themselves.

Effective execution of a goal starts with narrowing down the focus, and concentrating on what to focus on, despite many attempts by opposing parties to knock you off your stride. At the end of the day, if you do not yet know what needs to be done to achieve your ultimate aim, nothing else you achieve really matters that much.

2. Act only on the important goals.

When you already have your goals in place, you are in focus and know what to do to achieve those aims. Before you reach those goals, there will be many other small goals to achieve that may slow you down, keep you off track and use up whatever time you have to achieve that ultimate aim.

Act only on the lead measures. That means back to step one – the ultimate goal at hand. The Pareto principle states that 20% of activities produce 80% of the results. Track and identify the highest activities that need to be done and translate them into individual actions that you must track and observe periodically. That means whatever you are doing, you must know which goal is ultimately more important and ensure nothing keeps you from achieving it. The key here is prioritizing your principal activities so that the actual target stays in focus and on track.

3. Periodically review your goals.

When you have already set goals, it is imperative to know how long it is taking to achieve them, what you need to do and what to do if you fall behind schedule.

> *"You can do what I cannot do. I can do what you cannot do. Together we can do so many great things"*
>
> *– Mother Teresa –*

There will be times when you are not able to achieve what you have set out to do. Do not sulk but know exactly why you have failed and not achieved what you have set out to. Was it because there were other menial tasks that distracted you from the ultimate goal? Was the goal you have set up impossible to achieve in the time frame given? Asking questions like these are important so that we do not get buried in huge expectations while the goals are just impossible to achieve. When you set up goals that are unrealistic, you end up disappointing yourself and losing sight of what you have set up to do.

Therefore, the key word here is review, review and review! Have the courage to change the goal if need be. Ensure that proper justifications are made to support your decision, so that at the end of the day, no goal is big enough and goals are realistic, with resources in place.

4. **Create a sense of accountability among team members**

   Strong leaders or great performers thrive in a culture of accountability and responsibility for the tasks that they have been assigned to, for the results they achieve, be they good or bad. They should not shy away from defeat but pick themselves up and try harder at the next attempt. This is how a team can move forward more strongly and team spirit will improve. To achieve all this, the team must engage in frequent periodic assessment of their tasks, the goals at hand and analyze the path to move forward.

Constant feedback sessions to highlight the success of the team are essential to continually motivate staff. Analyze failures in a positive light with constructive corrective measures to create a sense of performance management system. In this way, the team will know clearly what they need to do to avoid negative recurrences in future.

There are thousands of ways to achieve better and stronger team work, but at the end of the day, if the goals of the team are not spelt out clearly, none of the ways matter since none of the members are clear on what they need to do.

Effective Communication Is Key

Communication is a process of interaction that allows two or more individuals to exchange information and ideas through several methods. Exchange requires feedback from both or all parties. Constructive feedback and ideas can be achieved through brainstorming sessions.

When a message is not properly communicated, the actual meaning is lost in translation, and as a result, the message sender blames the other person when things go wrong. How many times have you faced that situation only to realize that the message could have been better communicated in the first place? How many times have you ordered a chicken steak only to have the waiter serve you beef steak? It goes without saying, that if you want your team to jive and have cohesion, first and foremost, the goals that are set must be communicated clearly. The leaders and each member of the team must communicate each other's expectations clearly, leaving no stone unturned.

Let me share with you a simple joke that illustrates how important communication is. A man had a bitter argument with his wife and were both giving each other the silent treatment. Suddenly, the man realized that he needed his wife to wake him up at 6 a.m. the next day for an important business trip. Not wanting to be the first one to speak and hence lose the argument, he wrote on a piece of paper to his wife, "Please wake me up at 5 a.m., thanks" and left the note where he knew she would not miss it. The next morning, he woke up to find it was already 9.30 a.m. Furious, he went to find his wife to see why she had not woken him up as requested. He found a note next to his bed that read, "Wake up, it's 5 a.m."

There are two ways to say things, a good way and a bad way. Always learn to say something in the good way.

The point is, if there is no effective communication between two parties in agreement, most likely the results that you get will not be agreed upon no matter how hard one tries to be smart. Effective teams have teammates who are constantly talking to one another.

Call Centre Experience

About a year and a half ago, I joined a newly formed call centre that had been transferred to Malaysia. Over the next six months or so, the project was in a mess as it experienced some serious, 100% attrition. Service rating scores plummeted to levels never seen before, sometimes even to single digit percentage points by the end of the day. Our boss was in big trouble trying to get the project up and running.

The employees, me included, could not help but become affected by this situation. Morale in the camp was abysmal, to say the least. Cooperation was non-existent. The assistant managers each worked in their own styles and staff were confused about which style to follow. Communication was at an all time low. Each individual was just assuming what the other person was thinking and got along hoping things will turn for the better. After 15 months, the manager in charge of the project was removed, and in came another manager. As with each new change, I was hoping things would get better. The manager seemed to know her tasks well, but again, communication from manager to assistant manager, to staff on the floor, was lacking. Each of us assumed that we were doing the right thing and continued doing things the way they had previously been done.

As a result, the service level got very bad, attendance and schedule adherence was at an all time low, and people were calling in sick before and after their off days just to avoid coming to work.

The new manager had an even shorter stint than the first manager. After six months, the management decided to remove her. Another manager came in with renewed cause for change. Employees who had been there since the first manager, including me, were pessimistic about what further change the new man could bring. Some employees wondered how a company with a lousy product service, dissatisfied employees, low salary and a history of ineffective management (not once but twice!) could change.

The first thing the newest manager did when he came in was to change the culture of the company. Old and seasoned employees had gotten so used to the lack of communication and were blatantly calling in sick whenever they wanted. He removed these employees and hired new people with a fresh outlook. Next, he called for an emergency meeting with all the assistant managers and removed all our existing responsibilities and provided us with fresh ones. He insisted that we have meetings every week with each of our teams, no matter rain or shine. Next, he made it compulsory for each assistant manager to have at least a 30-minute weekly session with each of his/her staff on their team as well. We all got to work and proceeded to do as told. In the two months that followed, attrition was reduced tremendously and MC rates went down amazingly from 15% to 3-5% daily, in a 60 people workforce team. Productivity increased and service started to go up to a much more appropriate level than it was 6 months ago.

In short, our manager made it very clear that communication was vital to getting the message across. He knew if he could win the communication battle, he would get the employees' morale up again so they could work together for the good of the team, customers and ultimately the whole department concerned. Now, everyone is so excited to come to work and looks forward to the weekly meetings to share their thoughts and feedback on how best they can contribute to the team with their creative ideas. He turned the team around, with effective communication.

For leaders, always remember that your communication style sets the benchmark for the rest of your team members. Ensure that your communication style is consistent, clear and courteous. Always mean what you say. Walk the talk. In time, your staff will know that you mean business and that they can depend on you. Teams always reflect their leaders, as in "like father like son", "like member like leader". Good communication is never one way. The best teams always listen and encourage participation.

Being part of the team not only helps us achieve a sense of camaraderie, but also a sense of belonging to a group. We can also feel a sense of accomplishment, where two or more individuals are capable of achieving a task greater than any of us can achieve individually.

VII
ACCOUNTABILITY, INTEGRITY AND RESPONSIBILITY

"With great power comes greater responsibility."

– Uncle Ben from Spiderman –

This chapter deals with three of the most important words that many people will find in their entire lives. These words may seem simple, yet the impact on our lives is so significant and should be treaded on properly. Their effect on individuals, companies and organizations is so great, that if not understood properly, may result in negative repercussions for those involved.

Integrity

Integrity is defined in the dictionary as the quality of being honest and having strong moral principles. It is also defined as the state of being whole, unified and not divided. When

> *"When wealth is lost,*
> *nothing is lost.*
> *When health is lost,*
> *something is lost.*
> *When character is*
> *lost, all is lost"*
> *– Billy Graham –*

you have integrity, your words and your actions match. They are consistent with each other. You act on what you say, no matter where you are or who you are with.

When you act with integrity, you do not have to try so hard. You do not have to make people like you. In fact, you do not care if they like you or not. You can live and justify the decisions that you have made, and if the decisions are wrong, you know you will learn from the mistakes, get up and try again. You can live with yourself because you know you have acted in good faith, the actions have come from the heart and with love, and that is why we know them to be true.

Have you ever done something using an unorthodox or unconventional method, for which people around may have considered you weird, or have even advised you against using the method? Well you are not the only one. There are many out there who use creative ways, methods out of the norm to get what they want.

Mohandas Karamchand Gandhi was one such person. He was a leader, a motivator who inspired millions of people to fight for their freedom and their rights through a method that advocated the use of non-violent resistance. He successfully led India to independence and inspired people around the world.

He experienced many hardships during his lifetime. Once, he was rejected and forced to go from a first class train

> "When I despair, I remember that all through history the way of truth and love has always won. There are tyrants and murderers and for a time they seem invincible, but in the end, they always fall – think of it, always."
>
> – Mahatma Gandhi –

seat to a third class seat, even though he had a valid first class ticket. He was also beaten by a driver for refusing to travel on foot to make way for a European passenger. All these events have been turning points in his life, prompting him to fight racism, further prompting him to become a social activist later on in his life. It was through witnessing first hand prejudice and injustice against Indians in South Africa that Gandhi began to question his people's status within the British Empire, and his own place in society. He also knew that he had a responsibility towards the people of India.

Non-cooperation and peaceful resistance were Gandhi's weapons against the oppression of the British Empire at a time where acts of violence were rampant in India.

At times, when it seems you are fighting for a lost cause, do not despair if you know what you are doing is right. Keep fighting on, and I promise you will see the truth at the end of the day. A great leader may not always make the right decisions. But a great leader will always stand by his people, no matter how fraught the journey is, no matter how impossible the task may seem. He will never abandon them at a time when they need him the most. A true leader is indeed a person with integrity.

Integrity also comes with humility and selflessness as we act for the benefits of all parties involved and not just for ourselves. We have a sense of righteousness in what we are doing and know that the decisions that we make, no matter how painful they may seem at the time, serve to make this place a better place for all.

Integrity is included in this chapter because to achieve what you want (in the preceding chapters), to be an effective leader, to believe in what you can achieve, to motivate and inspire yourself and the masses, to achieve your goals (regardless of whether they are long or short term), you need to be steadfastly honest with yourself and others while executing the processes or plans that you have made through your analysis. Otherwise, you will not be successful and people will not follow you if you have no credibility. You can be the top manager in your company, a genius in your class, the best in what you do, but people will not care how much you know until they know how much you care.

Credibility means having the quality and the life values that make people believe or trust you. The more credible you are, the more confidence people have in you, and the more things you are able to get done. You will be able to get people to follow you when you suggest a new idea or when you want to place changes into their lives. It is often said that if you want to change an organization, change its leader. When you have integrity and credibility, your self image as an individual improves. When asked about you, people will give their interpretation – their perception and image they have of you. But remember, image is what people think you are, while integrity is what you really are. So whether it is true or not, it depends on your credibility and integrity.

Why Is It Important To Have Integrity?

According to a survey, we capture daily 89% of what we learn through our visual sensory system: that means from what we observe to be true and how we perceive things to be. The other 10% is captured through our audio sensory system: what people tell us, what we hear on the radio, the media and the likes; and 1% through other sensory means. That means if your subordinates observe what you say and what you do are the same, the results are consistent.

For instance, if you say that coming to work on time is important and you come to work on time, your employees will observe that trait in you and indirectly will follow suit. As the old saying goes, like father like son. In this case, like employer, like employee. However, if you say that coming to work on time is important and they often perceive that you come to work late or go home early, some of your employees will be on time, some will be late. They will be confused as to why a certain set of instructions are given, and a different set of actions are being carried out. Try it out. I have personally tested this at the workplace for little things like showing up on time and greeting all the staff. It works. How employees and subordinates behave reflects on how that team manager behaves. Therefore, if you want to know how good a manager or a leader is, look no further than the subordinates that he has.

Integrity Builds Confidence In People

When you walk the talk, people respect and admire what you say because they know that you will deliver. They know that if you have committed and given your word, no matter how hard the task is, you will complete it. This will garner respect and admiration for the leader. Therefore, when you lead, people will follow. Before people buy into the vision and ideas of the leader, they must buy into the leader and believe that he is sincere in helping them grow. In order to do that, the leader must have integrity as one of his values.

When people's confidence in you grows, they will trust that whatever you do will be in good faith towards them. They do not spend unnecessary time questioning the decisions that you have made, they do not question if your actions are without integrity and suspect that you have an ulterior motive. In other words, they have absolute confidence in what you have said and absolutely trust you. Most people look at positions or titles and think that with a higher position, the more integrity one has and the better one can lead a team. What is in a position? What is in a title? It is not a position or a title that makes that person. It is that person who makes that position or title. Often when people lack authority, they cannot be effective because they lack integrity. What they say does not hold up to what they do.

Integrity Influences And Inspires

Did you know that no matter what position you hold in your life or who you are as an individual or how insignificant you think you are, every single day when you interact with people, you potentially influence and inspire them directly or indirectly?

If you are a salesman, when you make a sales call, you influence your potential customer to buy a product or a service which you think can benefit him. You tell him about the advantages of the product or service, and if he buys, you will create an impact in his life, by having him use your product or service.

If you are a tourist guide, you have the potential to influence the perception of tourists that visit your country by taking them to places of interests to impress upon them what a great country this is. And how you treat them will directly give them the perception of the kind of people we are in this country. How many times have you heard of tourists complaining about the terrible attitude of taxi drivers in Malaysia, and how they overcharge tourists? I am not saying that all taxi drivers are like that. But think about it, each individual has the power and the potential to influence and inspire someone at some level.

If you are a father, what you do on a daily basis, how you set ground rules for your children, will deeply affect them when they grow up. How many of you out there have your father as a hero, someone whom you deeply admire and respect? I have often heard of daughters who want to find husbands or boyfriends with similar traits to their fathers. The list of examples is endless.

Integrity Creates Solid Reputation
And Lasting Image

Why is it that the advertising industry is such a booming business, supplying billions of dollars in revenue for companies worldwide? Why is it that people are willing to pay so much for good self image? The answer lies in integrity. Integrity creates long lasting images in people's minds and builds reputation for companies so that when people see a model image, they immediately remember the companies' products and services.

Companies are willing to pay millions of dollars to superstars like Roger Federer, Tiger Woods, David Beckham, just to endorse their products because these people serve as role models and inspiration to others out there. What they do, people follow. We have heard many times of million-dollar endorsement deals being cancelled because actors are caught driving under the influence of alcohol, or get arrested for speeding or minor traffic offences, or other criminal activities of the like. The truth is, nobody likes a person without integrity, and neither do we want to be associated with them. Hence, companies and large organizations cannot afford to have these superstars be suspect and lack integrity endorsing their products.

Prior to each election campaign, politicians hold rallies with shows of integrity and promises of what he or his party will do should they win the election, so people will vote for them. This is why, when news on the dirty linen of a potential candidate leaks, their integrity image suffers and all past image building, no matter how effective, will have been for nothing. As a result, the candidate is sure to lose in the election.

Ask yourself: are the results consistent with your actions? Are you the same person no matter who you are with? Do you make decisions that are mutually beneficial to others when another choice would benefit only yourself? Do you take credit for what others do? Your answers will reflect the degree of integrity and credibility that you have.

Life has its ups and downs. At times it will squeeze us and push us into a corner. It is at these times that the decisions we make can determine whether we are persons of integrity. Remember that image often produces much but integrity will always stand out.

Integrity Means Living It In Your Heart Before Inspiring Others

You can only lead a team as far as you have been yourself. You cannot expect your team members to go further than what you expect them to achieve. If you do not believe it in your heart, you will not be a great source of inspiration for others. No matter how much you emphasize something, people will be able to see through you, and the fact that you lack the conviction, lack the belief and most important of all, your actions do not match up to what you have said. That is, you lack integrity on what you have committed to.

When we carry out an action plan or develop a product, there are no shortcuts as far as quality is concerned. When integrity is involved, the truth will always prevail. In quality control, the end result is of no concern to the department assigned to carry out tests. The process of making the product is of higher importance than the end result. When the process is not followed properly, and if shortcuts are taken to develop the product, or corners are cut, then the end result of the product will be flawed. The same holds true for integrity, it guarantees credibility and brings out the best in you.

Have you seen a swimming coach who does not know how to swim? Or a driving instructor who does not know how to drive? Unlikely. Before you are able to inspire others to follow in your footsteps, they must know that you believe in your actions, and have the know-how and expertise to follow through. This is even more so when the going gets tough.

List out what you value in life, such as a belief that you are willing to fight for, or principles that you have always followed and mirrored through vital decisions in your life. What are your convictions? Ask someone who knows you well what areas they see as your strengths and what areas they see as inconsistent, or areas that you need improvement on.

When you reach a T-junction in life, it is time to make a decision. If that decision is a wrong one, it is important that you are aware of it and make the necessary adjustments to turn back. Otherwise, that decision may cost you something that you will regret later. Everyone will make wrong turns once in a while in their lives. What matters is when that time comes, you have the courage to turn back and start again.

Accountability

To be accountable means to be responsible for your decisions and actions, and you are expected to explain them when required. Accountability can be an abstract value to measure. What is accountable for you may not be so for others. How do you feel when someone makes you accountable for a task? Do you feel pressured to perform your best? Most people view accountability as something that pinpoints their mistakes or magnifies what they have done, most likely something that is negative. Many people think that accountability only crops up when something goes wrong or when there is a finger pointing at someone to blame. Notice that when things are sailing smoothly rarely do people ask, "Hey, who did this marvelous job in getting the birthday party started?" or "The person who organized this party should be given full credit for its success". Most of the time, we see people eager to take credit for work done by others, and shy away from taking any accountability and responsibility when things go wrong. Sadly, that is the reality in the world today.

What we know about the accountability value could not be further from the truth. The way we define accountability in our own dictionary will predetermine how our subconscious mind reacts when disaster strikes, when your loved one needs you to be the bigger person and whether you will be that person accountable for it.

Consider this new definition of accountability: a choice, a self-conscious decision to rise above mediocrity and demonstrate the responsibility and ownership necessary to achieve the desired results no matter how tough the odds are. This new definition gives new insight into ourselves from which we continually ask ourselves: what can we do better on this task to achieve the desired results, so that the next person who undertakes this task finds it a fraction easier than before, because of our contribution? Now take that for an accountability definition!

To create a culture of accountability where everyone wants to be accountable and responsible for the good reasons as well as for the bad, you need to clearly define what goals you want to achieve, be they personal, for family, a team or an organization. When the goals are outlined specifically and acknowledged by everybody involved, people feel that they are part of the team and want to work towards that common target. Everyone must know their roles, no matter how minor their actions are, which contribute towards the team's achievement.

Very often, accountability is a joint effort, a team game. Joint accountability occurs when everyone in the company assumes responsibility for the end result, the bigger picture. There is no personal glory, nor personal victory at stake, as far as joint accountability is concerned. It is highly unlikely that an individual can claim that he has done his or her job when the company has not achieved the overall objective or the desired result. Joint accountability simply means that everyone in the team becomes accountable for producing the results required.

Accountability For The Future

Only when you assume full responsibility for your thoughts and your desires, can you direct your own future and create your own destiny. If you do not plan for your future, it will most likely fall into someone else's plan.

To a certain extent, individuals with a high level of accountability can influence events before they happen. They can influence results in a positive way so much that they can anticipate what is going to happen before it happens! Isn't it powerful?

You can determine your own future by first creating values that only you can be accountable for. Your actions determine what you were before, what you presently are and what you can become in the future. Only when you are consistently aware of what you are doing, what you need to do and be accountable for, can you truly achieve what you want in your life, personally, spiritually, emotionally, financially, or socially and so on and so forth.

Responsibility

Responsibility is defined as a position, or a role of great or major accomplishment to assume the consequences, be they good or bad. It is a commitment and a duty. Different individuals have different sets of responsibilities in their lives and each bears an essential outcome of how their lives can be influenced, how in turn they can influence others. Responsibility as a parent is to ensure that your children get the best care possible, the best education, and the best childhood. To be the best parents is one of the core responsibilities of parents in our society. Responsibility as a student is to ensure that the teachings of your teachers and lecturers are best absorbed and applied in working life long after you have graduated. Responsibility as an employee in an organization is to ensure that you give your best in the tasks that you are assigned to, to the projects that you are allocated to, to the staff and subordinates that you are assigned to manage, and of course, to your line manager who is crucial for yourself and others around you.

These are examples of the responsibilities that we, as individuals face in our lives, sometimes oblivious to the influence that we bring to others when we make a decision. Since you know the immense impact you have on others, how can you influence others to do better? You may want to think twice before you tell off your fellow employees because of some uncontrollable emotional outburst.

Have you ever believed deeply in something that no matter what people tell you, you would stick to your beliefs? If you know what you stand up for is right and you are determined to stay the cause, never ever let anyone tell you otherwise. It is true that some mean well, and may not want you to suffer more than what you already have. Remember this however: a kite can only fly when it is thrown against the wind.

Nelson Mandela, one of the greatest leaders of all time, has fought for equal rights for all the people in South Africa. He was the leader engaged in resistance against the ruling party's apartheid policies after World War II. Born in 1918, he went on trial for treason in 1956-1961 and was acquitted in 1961.

In 1963, Mandela was again arrested for attempting to overthrow the government with the use of violence. He was found guilty and sentenced to life imprisonment. Not giving up, during his time in prison, his reputation grew steadily and became more and more influential, even though he was behind bars. He was widely accepted as one of the most prominent black leaders in South Africa and became a potent symbol of resistance as the anti-apartheid movement gathered momentum. He consistently refused to compromise his political position to gain his freedom.

After his release, more than 20 years later, he continued his life's work, striving to attain his goals that he and other prominent leaders set out nearly four decades ago. And in 1991, he was elected president of South Africa. Mandela made it his responsibility that the people of South Africa would never be ruled under apartheid policies and he made sure that this stayed true, no matter how long it took.

So, when you set up goals for yourself and others to achieve, you may not immediately see the results. Sometimes, you may deviate from your path to your goals due to some unforeseen circumstances. When that happens, set a revised target for your goals. Analyze what went wrong and make sure you do not repeat the mistakes. In that way, not only do you learn from your past experiences, but you become wiser and get better satisfaction when you attain your original goals. Persevere no matter how hard the journey or how impossible the task may seem.

When we take personal responsibility for the actions and the decisions we make, we are admitting that we are the ones responsible for the choices we make, not other people or events beyond our control. Let me emphasize this once more. Me, myself and I are responsible for the way I think and feel, not others. In the informative world that we live today, we may be influenced or swayed by the various media available, by people closest to us, or by people who have ulterior motives. However, only you have the final say, only you make the final decision. And only YOU control your own mind based on the analysis and information that you have gathered from external parties. Do not ever forget that! Nobody has the right to influence you to make a decision if you do not allow them to.

Let us now look at responsibility from your own view. Are you perfectly happy with the way things are going for you at the moment? Think about any aspects of your life. Do you like the way you do your reports? Do you like the way you procrastinate painting your room? Chances are you are neither happy nor extremely unhappy. You could be satisfied, but acknowledge that things can be a lot better if certain decisions or actions are taken. If you are not satisfied, then what are you doing about it? If you continue to accept things the way there are, everything will remain the same.

If you accept that weighing 250 pounds is alright or if you feel that your partner having an extra marital affair is acceptable and you do not do anything about it, nothing will change. If you realize that change in your life is warranted, the quality of your life should improve. Your present situation is not the result of your luck, your genes, your education, your parents, your health or anything else that you may have previously blamed for getting into this sticky situation. Recognize that you have the power, tools, support and the discipline necessary to change things into the way YOU want them to be. How? By first taking responsibility for the decisions and choices that you make. Understand that it is the choices you have made and the actions you have taken that brought you to where you are today. It was the decision to study law after graduating from high school that prompted you to practice law today. It was your decision to ask the girl out three years ago that resulted in holding her hand today. Whether that decision was right or not, only YOU can decide the next move.

With your thoughts you shape your decisions, with your decisions you shape your actions, and with your actions you shape your own destiny. Start by asking what type of responsibility or how much responsibility to take. Take a personal inventory of the things that are already under your care and the decisions that you make on a daily basis.

Do you often ask yourself these questions: "Life is so unfair, why am I so unlucky?", "Why are bad things always happening to me?", or tell yourself: "I am the way I am because my parents are divorced", or "My spouse is not supportive enough". If you answer "There is nothing I can do", then this is just the way your life will be for the next 20 years.

The questions above express the mindset of a self-made victim. Instead of taking personal responsibility, you conjure up similar thoughts to make yourself feel better for the things that you could not achieve, for the failed marriages and for the failed interviews. It is always easy to blame others for things that we cannot do and shift the responsibilities and burdens to other people to make us feel better. But until we start taking responsibility for the things that are happening to us, be they good or bad, we will not be making any real progress in our lives. Know that only you can hold yourself back, only you stand in your own way. You can change the way you live, the way you are by first simply changing the way YOU think.

By accepting responsibility to transform, you unleash the great power of your mind and take hold of our own destiny. By accepting the responsibility, you hold the power to make the right choices, the right decisions to improve your own life and to serve others selflessly. You achieve what you want in your life by helping others achieve what they want in their lives.

If you have been through bad times like the loss of a beloved close relative, saddled with poverty, and deprived of the many material things most people take for granted, do not despair. Instead, use these experiences as a challenge to look forward to a positive change in your frame of mind. Take action to change what you want to see happening right now at this very moment!

Let me illustrate an experience I had some time ago. I was at a playground once where many children were playing. Their parents were watching over them while reading their favorite magazines and books. People of all ages were there and were having a lot of fun. Suddenly, the clouds gathered, the skies darkened and soon after, it started pouring. All of a sudden, everybody started running for shelter, including myself, covering ourselves with anything we could find. One elderly man soaked to the skin was walking steadily from the playground to a nearby shelter. When he reached the shelter, a kid asked him, "Why are you walking so slowly when it's raining so heavily?" He looked at the kid and smiled, "It is raining up ahead as well". The point I am trying to make is not to worry about things you cannot change. A problem without a solution is not a problem. It is a fact that nobody can change, so why worry about it?

What if you knew when you were going to die? Three months from now, you would not be able to wake up and smell the fresh air, tell your children that you loved them or even do the things that you love. Would you accept death with open arms?

Randy Pausch was diagnosed with terminal pancreatic cancer. A smart, good-natured professor at the Carnegie Mellon University, he tried multiple treatments including chemotherapy until doctors confirmed that the cancer was terminal and he had only 3-6 months left to live. Thereafter, he started planning for his family's future. He went on to give his last lecture, *Really Achieving your Childhood Dreams* in September 2007. Before he started the lecture, over 400 students, professors and the like gave a standing ovation to an individual who had contributed so much to the world of technology. But he shrugged it off and replied to the crowd, "Make me earn it".

It is truly amazing to see individuals that are selfless and are still so eager to serve the people around them and the world even though they know tomorrow they will not be there to watch their teachings being passed on to others. These people are truly inspirational and set a good example of what is possible, and never to give up, even when you know you are going to die. I am sure that in his lifetime, Pausch achieved far greater things than most people ever did, or ever dreamed of achieving.

He said it best when he mentioned, "It is not about how to achieve your dreams. It is about how to lead your life. If you lead your life the right way, the karma will take care of itself". How true.

Pausch has also advocated teamwork and believed that you can only get to where you want through teamwork. If you are selfish to focus on yourself and not others, the journey to any of your goals will be slow, if at all possible. One of Pausch's childhood dreams was to play in the NFL. He did not make it.

There are things and goals that we are not able to achieve in our lifetime, due to circumstances beyond our control. But in hindsight, knowing that there may be a silver lining in what we could not achieve, more often than not, the lessons learned when we fail are often more valuable than those had we succeeded.

When we take personal responsibility for our own happiness, we relieve others of the burdens of our own expectations. In order for us to take responsibility, we need

> *"Experience is what you get when you didn't get what you wanted"*
> — Randy Pausch —

to know that we are responsible for all our emotions, be they happiness, sadness, fear, anger, excitement, ecstasy and so on. Try this little test. Think of something that has made you extremely happy in the past. Be as detailed and specific as possible. You will realize that the emotions of happiness, excitement and anything that relates to that experience will suddenly overwhelm you. You will feel energized and excited. Do it all over again and you will see a difference in your physiology.

Now think of something that has made you angry and bitter. It could be at work where you have overheard your colleague gossiping about you, or it could be a previous bad decision that you have made. You will notice that feelings of anxiety, nervousness, and anger start creeping in your mind. You may even start to tremble, and your heart starts beating faster.

See how powerful our mind is? With constant reinforcement of positive thinking and experiences, we can ultimately free our emotions from negative thinking and propel ourselves to a better living. What better way to start than to realize that we are responsible for our emotions, feelings and of course, well being. Recovering your personal power or positive thinking is not merely an intellectual exercise of the mind, but rather, you should treat it as a responsibility that requires action to change and develop your goals, habits and your points of view. With enough personal responsibility, you can change your entire self, physiologically and physically. You are responsible for everything in your dream, and that gives you the power to change it!

Victor Frankl, a renowned therapist and physician, wrote: "Everything can be taken from a man but one thing: the last of the human freedom – to choose one's attitude in any given set of situation, to choose one's own way".

In short, positive attitude or personal responsibility is the one thing that we possess that can never be regulated, taxed, stolen or taken away from us, unless we allow it to be.

I truly hope that the examples in this chapter are sufficient to impress upon you that you can be what you want to be, you can do what you want to do and you alone are in charge of your own destiny. I would like to end this chapter with a poem from an inspirational writer Margaret Fishback Powers, from her book *Footprints*:

I was walking along the beach with my Lord.
Across the dark sky flashed scenes from my life.
For each scene, I noticed two sets of footprints
in the sand, one belonging to me
and one to my Lord.

When the last scene of my life shot before me,
I looked back at the footprints in the sand.
There was only one set of footprints.
I realized that this was at the lowest
and saddest times of my life.
This always bothered me and I questioned
the Lord about my dilemma.

*"Lord, you told me when I decided to follow You,
You would walk and talk with me all the way.
But I'm aware that during the most troublesome
times of my life there is only one set of footprints.
I just don't understand why, when I needed
You most, You leave me."*

*He whispered, "My precious child,
I love you and will never leave you,
never, ever, during your trials and testings.
When you saw only one set of footprints
it was then that I carried you."*

POSTWORD

> "Everyone is an
> impossibility until
> he is born"
> – Ralph Waldo
> Emerson –

Well there you have it, an insight on how you can achieve anything that you want if you only believe you can get it. I wish you have benefited at least one or two things after reading this book. Hopefully, this book can enable you to strive to become a better individual, a better person collectively and of course enjoy reading it in the process. If you have come this far and completed reading this book, surely by now you know the message that I am trying to drive through; you have the ability and power to control what you think, want and do.

I wish you continued success, continued excellence in whatever endeavour that you do. Pursue your dreams. Pursue your goals and remember never to give up until you get what you set out for. Everyone wants to achieve something in their life. It may be in terms of financial goals, emotional goals, relationship goals, career goals; anything at all. Ideas, dreams and goals when translated into specific plans of action, are the beginning of all successful achievements.

Remember, you can live the life you want by changing the way you think. You are here on this earth for a reason, and this world needs what you have to offer. So stop wasting anymore time and do what you know you have to do.

References And Suggested Reading

Covey, Steven R., *The Seven Secrets of Highly Effective People*, FreePress, 2004.

Hill, Napoleon, *Think Rich, Grow Rich*, Napoleon Hill Associates Creative Vision Sdn. Bhd., Malaysia, August 2005.

Khoo, Adam, *Master Your Mind, Design Your Destiny*, Adam Khoo Learning Technology Group Pte Ltd, 2004.

Losier, Michael J., *Law of Attraction*, Wellness Central Edition, 2006.

Maxwell, John C., *Ultimate Leadership*, Thomas Nelson Inc., 2001.

Pausch, Randy with Jeffrey Zaslow, *The Last Lecture*, Hyperion, 2008.

Robbins, Anthony, *Awaken the Giant Within*, FreePress, Simon & Schuster, New York, 2003.

Robbins, Anthony, *Unlimited Power*, FreePress, Simon & Schuster, New York, 2003.

Schwartz, David J., *The Magic of Think Big*, Pocket Books, 2006.

W. Chan Kim & Renee Mauborgne, *The Blue Ocean Strategy*, Harvard Business School Press, 2005.

Welch, Jack, *Winning*, Harper Collins Publishers, 2005.

Ziglar, Zig, *Over The Top*, Thomas Nelson Inc., 1997.

Ziglar, Zig, *See You At The Top*, Pelican Publishing Company Inc., 2007.

THE AUTHOR

Elvin Vong is a self-motivated individual whose job is to train, motivate and inspire his subordinates to achieve higher results within the time line given, with limited resources.

He holds a degree in Bachelor of Computer Science, Majoring in Mathematics from the University of Tunku Abdul Rahman.

His position as one of the team managers in one of the largest contact centre in Malaysia, enables him to utilize everyday examples in this book to motivate and inspire his readers.

At 26, his success includes winning the excellence award (Consolation Prize) Best Contact Centre Team Leader; Open Category 2009 in the Contact Centre Awards Malaysia CCAM 2009.